"While taking us ... ers in wartime with her mother, ... ne of the many forgotten episodes in a long and cruel ... ea. So many so-called ordinary people endured extraordinary events that would test even the bravest of us to the limit and beyond. Too often it is the big episodes of war that are remembered and written about. In bringing so vividly to life the sinking of the liner S.S. Britannia by the notorious Nazi disguised raider Thor, Eleanor Stewart reveals not only her own incredible family history – and the amazing courage of her mum - but also makes us all wonder what we would do adrift in that lifeboat for days, surviving only on biscuits and condensed milk."

Iain Ballantyne author of *Killing the Bismarck*

"This book is as much about a parent's extraordinary back story as it is about a daughter who has tenderly pieced it together."

Jane Christmas, author of *Incontinent on the Continent*

"Eleanor Stewart introduces us to the adventures of her intrepid mother in a way that is sympathetic without being sentimental. Coming to understand our parents simply as human beings, as flawed and fragile as we know ourselves to be, is often the gateway to inner maturity, and even peace, which Eleanor demonstrates. As this humorous and personal tale unfolds, we not only voyage across the world, we also travel into the hearts of a feisty woman and her dedicated daughter."

Sharon Grenham-Thompson, author of *Jail Bird*

"This book is a terrific reminder that no life is ordinary. Starting with the frailty of her mother's old age, the author tells a story of adventure, tragedy and immense courage. Once started, you won't want to put it down."

Gethin Russell-Jones, author of *My secret life in Hut 6* (with Mair Russell-Jones) and *Conchie*

*To the memory of all those who lost
their lives at sea during the Battle of
the Atlantic, and to the memory of my
mother, who survived*

ELEANOR STEWART

A Voyage Around My Mother

SURVIVING SHELLING, SHIPWRECKS, AND FAMILY STORMS

LION

Published by Lion Books
an imprint of
Lion Hudson plc
Wilkinson House, Jordan Hill Road,
Oxford OX2 8DR, England
www.lionhudson.com/lion

ISBN 978 0 7459 6883 4
e-ISBN 978 0 7459 6884 1

First edition 2016

Acknowledgments
Bible extracts are taken from The Authorized (King James) Version.
Rights in the Authorized Version are vested in the Crown. Reproduced
by permission of the Crown's patentee, Cambridge University Press.
Scripture quotation in chapter 19 is taken from the *Holy Bible, New
International Version*, copyright © 1973, 1978, 1984 International Bible
Society. Used by permission of Hodder & Stoughton, a member of the
Hodder Headline Group. All rights reserved. "NIV" is a trademark of
International Bible Society. UK trademark number 1448790.

A catalogue record for this book is available from the British Library

Printed and bound in the UK, September 2016, LH26

*All the characters and events in this book are true, as detailed by my mother
Mary Stewart (1911–2003) in her diaries and in the thirty hours of cassette
recordings she made in the 1980s. Many of the names have been changed to
protect the guilty.*

A delightful photograph of my mother Mary Stewart, aged about twenty-eight.

THE BRITISH BROADCASTING CORPORATION
Broadcasting House, London, W. 1
TELEPHONE: WELBECK 4468 TELEGRAMS: BROADCASTS, LONDON

Extract from the News, Sunday 15th June, 1941, 9.00 a.m.

Stories of the fortitude shown by British merchant sailors after their vessels had been sunk by enemy action are told in news agency messages this morning. Twenty-six survivors from the British steamship BRITANNIA have arrived in New York after spending twenty-three days in an open boat. Forty-four of the survivors died after they had taken to the lifeboats. The BRITANNIA was attacked by a raider with six-inch guns, and her crew of a hundred, with three hundred passengers, crowded into four open boats. One of the boats set course for South America, fifteen hundred miles away, and the men were rationed to an ounce of water and one biscuit a day. The remaining thirty-eight finally beached the boat at a point on the coast of Brazil. They were too weak to walk, and fell exhausted on the beach. Eventually the British consul made arrangements for the survivors to be taken to hospital. It is understood that, in all, about two hundred of those on board the BRITANNIA were saved.

Contents

Acknowledgments

I would like to acknowledge my husband's support and the help and encouragement of Ali Hull of Lion Hudson who has, with unfailing good humour, put up with my dreadful spelling and even worse punctuation.

Author's Note

Accounts of the sinking of the SS *Britannia* by the German surface raider *Thor* are documented on the internet and in *The Secret Raiders* by David Woodward.

Much of the dialogue in the book is verbatim. Some literary licence has been taken in the interests of style and continuity when a third-person narrative predominates.

Prologue

*O*n 25 March 1941 *Thor* intercepted the SS *Britannia*, an 8,800-ton British passenger ship. After scoring several hits on the fleeing ship *Kähler*, *Thor*'s captain allowed the SS *Britannia* to be abandoned before firing sixteen 15 cm (5.91 in) rounds into her waterline, sinking her.

German wireless operators intercepted a message from a nearby British warship approaching at full speed from about 100 nautical miles (190 km) away. *Kähler* decided not to risk encountering her, and reasoned that the British ship would arrive and assist those in the water. Unfortunately, the British warship failed to find the survivors. It was left, primarily, to *Cabo de Hornos, Bachi*, and *Raranga* to rescue about 285 of the passengers and crew aboard SS *Britannia* that actually took to the lifeboats. My mother was one of them. The rest, over 200 of them, perished.

Seventeen other survivors eventually reached land at Sao Luis, on the coast of Brazil, after twenty-three days and 1,500 nautical miles (2,800 km) adrift at sea.

1

Portsmouth:
Mother's Arrival (1993)

$\mathcal{T}$he news that my eighty-two-year-old mother had had "a funny turn" didn't come as a complete surprise, although I had expected a fall instead of a state of confusion where she didn't know who she was or where she lived.

"She shouldn't be living on her own, you know!" the bossy friend who had brought her home told me over the telephone. This "Good Samaritan" had been in the Post Office when the incident occurred and had taken my mother back to her flat, before contacting me.

Actually, my mother's Parkinson's symptoms weren't that bad. Her hands trembled, she could not type or knit any more, and when she was tired her head shook a little. She still managed to shop and to cook for herself; she had never lost the art of baking, and her scones and shortbread were the stuff of legend. I had feared a fall, first because of the little flight of steps down from her flat to the patio, and second because of the dreadful state of the pavements leading to George Street where she shopped.

My husband, John, and I talked the situation over, although with some trepidation on my part. My relationship with my mother had never been easy. Although I saw her very regularly, almost weekly, and she was a frequent visitor to our home, nevertheless it was a relief that we were forty miles apart. My brief experience of living with her as an adult in the past had not been successful, and I had some disquiet about us being under the same roof.

My brother Peter advised caution, but as he was not in a position to help, the alternatives were limited. Over the next week or so, John and I talked about it.

"I really don't know what else we can do! She's very frail and since the amnesia, I feel awful about her being on her own in Hove when we have plenty of room here. Although I do understand if you don't want to."

If my husband felt dismay or resentment, he hid it gallantly.

"I mean," I rushed on, "she likes her independence and I don't think she would accept an old folks' home – what a ghastly name that is – but she really needs to be closer or *I* need to be closer and clearly as we aren't going to move, she'll have to."

I knew I was beginning to babble and could feel my anxiety mounting.

And so it was decided. I think that John felt it difficult to refuse. We were already sharing a home with his parents, and with the children gone we undoubtedly had the available space.

Out of two big adjacent bedrooms, we created a bed-sitting room and a little kitchen-diner. With her bathroom next door she would be able to maintain her independence. "This is perfect," she announced, the day we moved her in. "It will be wonderful to have you so close." She looked delighted, smiling and enthusiastic.

"It'll be fine," I told John, that first evening. "She's settling down already, watching snooker." The cat immediately took up residence in her sitting room, something that charmed her. The house was large enough for the sound of her TV to be inaudible. This was just as well, as, with her usual obstinacy, she had initially refused to admit she was deaf. When finally she did accept it, she declared herself far too old to adapt to hearing aids, and consequently her radio and TV were always at maximum volume.

The only noticeable disadvantage, picked up immediately by Esme our daughter whenever she came home, was my mother's cigarettes. The smell permeated down into our kitchen. She was a twenty-a-day smoker. She clearly did not have the genetic disposition to lung cancer: she rarely had a cold; I never knew her to have a chest infection and I never ever heard her cough.

Apart from the smell of tobacco, there were few problems initially. She was able to walk along to the local corner shop only two or three minutes away, and the parish priest came to bring her Holy Communion every week.

Then about six months after her arrival and during John's absence visiting an aunt in Australia, she became very unwell with a mysterious viral infection, which caused severe cramps in all her limbs and had for a side-effect a really bad case of oral thrush. Her mouth was painfully sore and she visibly deteriorated. It was a struggle to get fluids into her and she ate almost nothing for a fortnight. Her weight dropped alarmingly (she was a tiny woman anyway) and she became both drowsy and restless. The doctor and the district nurse were not optimistic. I took to sleeping on a mattress, which I dragged into her room. At night she groaned and wept. Peter came over several times to spend the night and to allow me to get some decent sleep.

"I told John it won't be long," I said to him, as our mother faded in front of us. It was like nursing a small feverish child. Her illness caused me much greater distress than I expected. When her small, dry, claw-like hand clung to mine and I felt her head against my shoulder as I struggled to get some barley water or high protein liquid food into her, I felt overwhelmed with pity and even grief. Eventually the doctor prescribed oral morphine and synthetic saliva spray for her dry mouth. It gave her some relief from the pain on her tongue. She began to sleep better, her restlessness diminished, and slowly she began to improve.

One morning, I was helping her to drink some tea. She looked up at me and whispered, "Do you think I could have a wee cigarette?"

My goodness, I thought, *she's going to get better*! My burst of laughter was a mixture of relief and dismay. All that distress for nothing.

She made a good physical recovery, but my care of her made her lean increasingly on me. She never returned fully to the determined independence that she had manifested so feistily when she lived in Hove, and which she continued to show when she first moved in with us. She had always been an emotional creature and soon I was getting a great deal of pressure put on me to devote more time to her than I really was able to give. There was a great deal of "You're the only one I can talk to. You are the only one who understands." Occasionally she spoke about my father, Colin, her husband, usually with some bitterness. I think it was justifiable but it put me under considerable stress. I was always on the verge of reminding her how badly I thought *she* had behaved over my marriage, refusing to come to the wedding if my father attended.

Despite our rocky relationship, I loved her dearly, but I had a husband, and we had a business and a house to run. We also had an active social life and she would often show open displeasure if I curtailed any time with her because we were going out or had friends to stay. She had ceased to be at all gregarious and disliked "outdoors".

This was a major change in her personality, for I knew as a young woman she had been lively and loved company. So on a sunny evening, when John and I invited his parents to join us in the garden for a drink, something we did often, she would decline to join us, saying, "It's too cold" or "I don't like smoking outside." I got into the habit of going up to spend an hour with her at about 6 p.m. so my evenings with my husband were not interrupted. This meant that often I had to forgo the easy and comfortable time in the garden, leaving my family sitting happily in the sun, to return indoors to my mother. I would take a very serious whisky with me!

To John's dismay, I also began to smoke again. It was the one thing my mother and I could share. As her life was shrinking, we had less and less to say to each other. My life and what I had been doing didn't interest her in the least. She had a curious emotional detachment from her grandchildren, even when they were very small. She knitted for them and made Esme's school uniform, but there was little warmth in her interaction with them. Unlike my mother-in-law, she never offered to baby-sit for us. She had been extremely resentful if I had to break off a conversation with her in order to attend to a child. When we returned from some social event or holiday and told her about it, politeness demanded that she made the right noises: "That's nice, dear" or "I'm pleased you had a pleasant time", but I knew she was indifferent.

Then one evening she produced a box of cassette tapes. There were about twelve of them. I turned them over and looked at them. They were entitled "The way it was" and they covered her young life and her amazing and extraordinary wartime adventure. Suddenly I discovered that we would have something to talk about. She was pink with pleasure as I began to show an interest and became excited and animated. "I've got diaries too," she said, "and letters."

I realized that if I truly wanted her remaining years to be happy I had to give up all expectation that she would share my life and interests and instead enter hers.

"Tell me all about it. Every detail!" I said. And so she did.

2

Govan (1920s) *via Buffalo* (1930) *to Dunoon* (1932)

*S*he was spoiled at home. As the baby of the family with three elder brothers, one of whom was married by the time she was ten, she felt herself surrounded by adults. Her mother was always busy, but her father, Archie, indulged her. When she committed some misdemeanour, he would say, "She's only a wee thing. She didn'a mean it."

Born in 1911 after three sons, this pretty, vivacious child both enchanted and bemused him. Her brothers, too, were proud of her mischievous adventurous nature. John, the next eldest in age, would put her on the crossbar of his bicycle to take her to watch him play football in the local park. The eldest, Archie, named (inevitably in Scotland) after his father, bought her humbugs and sherbet lemons. Of the youngest brother, Hughie, more later.

At school she was a popular, hardworking pupil, but her lively sense of fun often landed her in trouble. Once, with time on her hands, she and a couple of fellow spirits found a terracotta bust of the Scottish poet Robbie Burns in the art room. Deciding to "improve" on it, they painted it in a variety of lurid colours and finished by tying a paint rag artfully round its head. They were so enchanted by their efforts that they felt compelled to share them.

A row of classrooms nearby had glass panels two thirds of the way down from the ceiling so as to improve the lighting of the room. Mary and friends dragged stools from the art room, piled them up and stuck the now polychrome Robbie Burns on the top. From this glass vantage point he peered dolefully down on the working pupils below! The teacher, with her back to the wall, didn't observe this masterpiece at first but the girls saw it immediately and there was an outburst of muffled giggling. The teacher burst from the classroom, Mary and her friends scattering before her. They shot into the toilets and dived into the cubicles. Two were hauled out immediately, but Mary, small and light, hung on to the hook inside the door and rested her toes on the ledge, so that when the cubicle door was pushed she swung inwards with it.

She might have got away with it, but the paint, still fresh on her hands, was noticed by the sharp-eyed teacher.

"Girl McCutchion," said this stern disciplinarian. "You're the essence of stupidity." And she strapped her twice across her palms!

Her mother, noting Mary's pink hands, was all for repeating the tawse but her father intervened. "Och now, Jane, it wasn't a so bad and she's had her punishment. Away out now, and play." He winked at her behind her mother's back, and Mary grinned back.

In the twenties, and despite the proximity of the docks, Govan was a quiet, respectable, working-class suburb of Glasgow, almost rural in parts. Its dire reputation for crime and drugs lay in the future. Her parents' flourishing vegetable garden gave out onto fields and at the end of the road there was a small farm and a burn. Mary wasn't supposed to play in the burn but her wet socks and shoes showed how often she defied that ban.

Archie McCutchion was a small, quiet man with soft brown hair and a neat moustache of which he was secretly extremely proud. He had a small brush to tend to it and sometimes he let Mary comb it through. She always tried to tease it into a "handlebar" but it remained stubbornly "walrus". Archie worked in the John Brown & Company shipyard on Clydebank as a design engineer. He had served an apprenticeship for this and was talented enough to have been sent to Venice as a young man to study ship design. Later he proudly told Mary that he'd worked on the *Lusitania*.

Despite protecting Mary from her mother's stricter regime, he was a loyal and loving husband, saying often to his children, "You must be kind to your mother. She has a hard time!" As he said this his voice would thicken with tears.

Jane McCutchion was a devoted parent but there was tragedy in her life. Her first pregnancy had been undiagnosed twins. Archie, the first-born, was perfect but Hughie's traumatic delivery forty minutes later left him brain-damaged. He never grew up. He could wash and dress and feed himself, but remained a permanent infant. He never went to school, but was still a smiling, loving, happy child.

Hughie was cosseted and adored by the whole family, but his mother reserved her special tenderness for him. He was subject to epileptic seizures. Sometimes if she saw the signs of an imminent fit, she could prevent them, or so she thought, by asking softly, "What is it, my son, my wee lad?" She would stroke his brow with infinite gentleness, and smile at him. She was fiercely protective, and once, when a well-meaning neighbour, looking with concern at her pale, worn face, said, "He ought to be in a home, Mrs McCutchion," Jane replied, with dignified fury, "He *is* in a home." She never spoke to the woman again.

Hughie died in 1928, at the age of eighteen, from continuous, uncontrollable convulsions. All the love in the world could not stop them. His mother refused to have his body removed from the house for four days, and would say to Mary, "We'll just have a look at your poor brother," taking her reluctant daughter into his room to look fearfully at his body. Mary never forgot the sweet smell of decay, a smell that her mother insisted was the lilies.

In 1930, Mary and her parents went to live in Buffalo, New York, in the United States, leaving behind her brothers and their families. Her father was offered a year's contract, with the option of making it permanent. It seemed a good change; something that would distract his wife from the grief of her son's death. They stayed with her father's cousin, a large strident woman called Aunt Bessie. Her husband, a thin colourless man, was in complete thrall to his wife and looked with astonishment at Mary's father when he asserted even the mildest authority over his own wife. He was even more amazed when she acquiesced. There was nothing conciliating about Aunt Bessie!

Mary went to college and was happy enough, though at home she had nothing in common with her aunt's stolid girls, who expressed unconcealed bemusement, even dismay, at the idea that there was to be pleasure in reading, one of Mary's passions. She thought them complete ninnies!

They stayed in Buffalo for a year, until the end of her father's contract. Jane McCutchion was pathologically homesick. She was very close to all her children and although she found son Archie's wife a little tiresome, she adored Lily, John's wife. She was a dark-haired, laughing Irish girl from Londonderry, who, together with her two brothers, formed a song and dance act at the Citizens Theatre in the Gorbals area of Glasgow. Lily brought glamour and laughter into their lives. Jane missed them all dreadfully and her husband gave in. Archie only ever wanted his family, and particularly his wife, to be happy. He reclaimed his previous job in the shipyard and the family returned to Scotland.

The house in Govan had been sold, so they moved to Dunoon, the charming seaside resort "doon the water" where they had spent summer holidays. They bought a large, pleasant flat next door to Aunt Jeannie, Mary's father's sister, whom Archie believed would be company for his wife. Aunt Jeannie was a spinster with an overwrought temperament, subject to fits of sudden and unexpected hysteria. Archie thought this "women's business" and, when not at work, absented himself on Saturday afternoon to indulge his enjoyment for bowls. When he retired, this became an all-consuming passion.

Initially, Mary was happy in Dunoon. Outgoing and friendly, she had made friends there during the holidays, and there were new ones to make. They swam, played golf and tennis, walked in the hills above the town, shopped in Gourock across the Clyde, or went to the cinema. In Dunoon she got her first paid job, working in the steam laundry.

More importantly, she fell in love. She'd had flirtations before, light-hearted affairs that never touched her heart. She acknowledged her ruthlessness when she tired of her suitors, several of whom were quite keen to marry her, dismissing them summarily but always managing to stay friends. But in 1936 she fell in love – really, truly, deeply in love. She later said she was never that much in love again.

Interlude

In the hours I spent sitting beside her in the evenings, my mother opened herself to me and I met a completely new person. We had never been completely estranged, but she had been hurt and affronted that her plans for us to live together after I left my convent, where, throughout my twenties, I had been a nun, did not correspond to my own desires. There had been coolness between us for a while. Eventually we had built some bridges, met regularly, and spent some holidays together, but I could never feel we were close.

Her episodes of poor mental health, all of which occurred when I was a nun, were undoubtedly exacerbated by my father's careless behaviour. The eight years I had spent in France and in Liverpool meant that I did not witness the deterioration of their marriage. I admired her for rebuilding her life but this happened in my absence and those eight years meant I grew from adolescence to womanhood, and she from early middle age to her sixties without us seeing much of each other at all. In some respects, I hardly knew her.

The tapes were a revelation. It was like watching a shadowy figure take on substance: flesh and bone. She had an intimate, lively delivery and, sometimes, even a melodramatic one, but her story had the ring of authenticity. What astonished me most was the detail of her recall. It was not just the events themselves – the time and place, gripping though these were – but she remembered conversations, the expressions on people's faces, what they were doing at a particular time.

I wondered if she embellished the stories. It would not have been unreasonable for her to have reworked certain memories. But she was adamant that it happened exactly as she told it. As to the tapes, she wanted me to listen to them on my own; she seemed oddly shy about my doing so in her presence. This had its advantages. It meant I could think about them, and thinking about them beforehand gave me reasons to ask for more details. So I dug deeper into her history, and was able to ask detailed questions that were more personal. Her past life was more immediate, it seemed to me, than her present existence, and she delighted in amplifying the things I listened to so avidly.

"Hang on," I'd say. "Don't stop. I'll put the kettle on and get another whisky."

This always made her laugh.

3

Dunoon:
Love and Sadness (1936)

The year of 1936 was a halcyon one for Mary. All through the warm summer days, she and Michael walked in the hills. When the weather was unsettled there were trips to the Kelvingrove Art Gallery in Glasgow, concerts and the cinema, and afternoon teas with buttered scones. There were long and loving plans for the future. For many years after, she was to remember it as a time of the most sublime happiness.

The afternoon he gave her the brooch, they had walked round the Bishop's Glen beyond the reservoir above the town. Afterwards they sat down in companionable silence. She stretched out on the ground, lying back with her hands behind her head. Through narrowed lids she watched the clouds scudding across the sky. Sometimes things rustled in the grass nearby: a beetle or an insect of some sort maybe. She was not alarmed; she was not the sort of girl to be afraid of spiders or creepy crawlies of any kind. There was a pleasant breeze coming off the surface of the water behind them, ruffling her hair and lifting her skirt a little. She knew it uncovered her knees but was too lazy to pull it down. The clouds drifted out across the Clyde, shimmering glassily below, and she felt the sun on her arms. She relaxed.

"Do you think we'll have rain tomorrow?" she asked Michael sleepily.

They were planning to walk to Hunters Quay and even Sandbank, and have tea at the hotel. They had been going out together for six months – "walking out; keeping company" was the local expression. He was Irish, blue-eyed, dark, and fiercely handsome, a teacher in Gourock, and five years her senior. From the moment she met him she had thought him exactly the kind of man she had been looking for: intelligent, articulate, fun. He teased her often, with a gentle mockery that both entranced and bewildered her, and, just as she was about to get cross, disarmed her by quoting from *Romeo and Juliet*: "Here's what love is. A smoke made out of lovers' sighs. When the smoke clears, love is a fire burning in your lover's eyes!" He made no secret right from the beginning that this was a courtship, and marriage was the object. She fell in love with him – desperately in love – almost straight away.

"I don't think it looks like rain," he said. Mary could tell by his voice that he was smiling. "We'll take macs if you are worried." She didn't answer. It was such a nuisance, she thought, to have to carry raincoats. After a pause, he added, "We'll risk it."

She felt the back of his fingers trailing along her arm. The heather beneath her rustled and, without opening her eyes, she knew he had lain down beside her. His caress stopped at her elbow and she wondered if he was going to kiss her, and turned her face hopefully. The kiss did not arrive. She opened her eyes to find him propped on his elbow looking down at her with an expression of great intensity.

She grew chilly despite the sun, thinking there would be a repeat of his patient but persistent queries. Instead, he said, "I've got something for you." When he brought out the little blue box, she was filled with apprehension knowing she would not be able to give him an answer to the question that she both dreaded and longed to hear. When she opened the box she was torn by a mixture of relief and disappointment. It was a brooch – a pretty amethyst stone set in a silver filigree thistle.

He leaned over her and pinned it on to her blouse, smiling. She touched it with her finger. "It's beautiful!"

"So," he said, "no awkward decisions today, my sweetheart." He spoke with some irony, knowing what she had expected, then he added, "Have you spoken to your parents again?"

So the persistent query had come after all.

She felt she ought to sit up to respond but thought it might invest the discussion with too much seriousness. If she stayed lying down and answered sleepily it might remain light-hearted. She knew this to be craven. He loved her; he had the right to an answer.

"Yes, I have." She rolled over to face him and he picked pieces of heather from her hair.

"Well?"

"I don't know," she sighed. "They seem as difficult." It wasn't the word she wanted. She wanted to say "obstinate, bloody-minded, prejudiced as ever". She recalled, with pain, her father's cold, closed face – he who was by nature a gentle, tolerant man – when she had told him of Michael, and her Aunt Jeannie's near hysteria. The family scene had been hideous.

"Heavens above, Papa, he's only a Catholic! You'd think he was a Satanist." Her Presbyterian father had given no answer, but turned away in silence and then left the house, "for a wee walk", he said. She had been so harrowed by it that she had only spoken in general terms about her family's opposition to their relationship. The whole thing was deeply unpleasant; the rows painful, the silences even worse.

She tried to explain to him. "Michael, listen. Up in the Isles, even further up in the Highlands, there are plenty of Catholics, but here on the West Coast, it's a bastion of Presbyterianism." She studied the planes of his face and put up her hand to touch his jaw, already dark and rough with his evening shadow. He took her hand and kissed the palm.

"They'll come round," she said. "They'll have to. They won't risk losing me." She sounded more confident than she felt.

He was silent looking down at the little town below. It was dappled in sun and shadow. Someone had a bonfire going and the grey smoke curled lazily up, drifting on the breeze towards them. He could smell it. "All my hopes and dreams are going up in smoke," he told her fancifully. He reached behind him for his jacket and pulled a packet of cigarettes from the pocket. He pulled out two, lit them both, and handed one to her. "Suppose they don't come around? Will you marry me anyway? Become a Catholic? Risk never talking to your family again?"

"Oh, Michael!" She put her arms around his neck, tears thick in her throat. "We don't need to talk about this today. My mother doesn't care *who* I marry as long as I am happy. I just wish she'd give me some support, but her generation never go against their husbands, even when they know they are wrong. My father can change his mind. Look, I didn't think he'd ever forgive me when I threw up the job at the laundry. He didn't speak to me for a week but then it all blew over. He actually thinks doing the bookkeeping and the salaries for the power station, now that Dunoon has electricity, is quite acceptable, even prestigious – a daughter that works in the offices of the new power station. If I present them with a *fait accompli*, what option do they have?"

He dropped the subject, wrapping his arms round her, and they smoked in tense silence, she leaning back against him until she felt him relax. She knew that his own parents were almost as dismayed by the relationship. He told Mary that he had determinedly ignored his mother's reproach. "Could you not have found a good Catholic girl? What about Isa Ferguson?"

"What did you say to that?"

"I just wasn't prepared to tolerate her interference. I told her that Isa Ferguson is stepping out seriously with Robbie McKay. I'm twenty-five and I'll find my own bride." Mary smiled: it all sounded so familiar.

If things were troublesome at home for him, they became almost intolerable for her. The common practice at that time, as she well knew, was for the unmarried daughter to stay at home to care for aging parents, or at least to remain within easy reach. Both her brothers were married and living in Glasgow. Mary saw her future mapped out for her. If marriage was inevitable, then her parents wanted a local lad. Nothing adventurous. Even Gourock was a stretch too far.

For Mary, the aura of vehement disapproval and her father's intransigence about her papist boyfriend was like an unhealed sore. She began to lie about when she met him. Their secret and guilty dates brought her personal anguish. She hated dissimulation.

Eventually, perhaps inevitably, worn down, like poor Anne Elliot in *Persuasion*, she bowed to the family pressure.

Michael reproached her with anguished bitterness on the autumn day when, with rain pouring down their riven faces, they parted. She stood, sodden, watching the ferry taking him away, as it disappeared across the water. Walking back to the family home, she felt a stiffening in her heart, leading to a resolve that she embraced with calculated determination. Never again would she be pushed against her judgment. Never again would she go against her heart. She would be her own mistress, decide her own destiny. All her decisions would be hers and hers alone.

Over the next few days, her father, anxiously but clumsily attempting to make amends, and distressed by her white face and drawn mouth, began to propose other employments. He suggested an opening in a local architect's office, or a secretary and accounts clerk for a builder's merchant. She ignored him, knowing he found her silence unnerving.

"I've made some plans. I'm going to London," she announced one evening. With quiet satisfaction, she saw both her mother's dismay and her father's horrified stare. Aunt Jeannie's hysterics she completely ignored. In her bedroom, she kissed Michael's amethyst brooch and then, sitting at her table, she finished the application letter to May & Baker Ltd, a pharmaceutical firm in Dagenham in Essex, who were currently advertising for secretarial staff.

Interlude

"Did you leave Dunoon to punish your parents?"

It seemed so obvious to me that she had done so. It was a fine evening, but I had failed to lure her out into the garden, where my husband and parents-in-law were having a drink, enjoying the last of the evening sun. I was resentful about this. I was missing social contact which she could have joined in but she wanted me to herself. So my question was a little harsher than usual.

She looked startled. "Heavens, no!" Then she hesitated. "Well, perhaps a little, but it wasn't so much that; I just knew I had to get away from Dunoon. With Michael gone, there was nothing to keep me there. But it was a huge change; scary really."

"You seem to remember all your times with him so vividly."

"I've never forgotten a single moment with him. I remember it all as if it were yesterday." She laughed as if embarrassed by the cliché. "I should have married him; he'd have made me happy. I wasn't strong enough to resist the family pressure, not brave enough."

To my dismay she began to cry very softly. I felt her pain quite clearly and didn't know how to comfort her. This sadness for a lost love moved me. I took her hand and stroked it. "Perhaps I didn't love him enough," she said quietly.

"It was hard for you in the face of your parents' intransigence. Sometimes love isn't enough, is it?"

We sat in silence for a moment or two then she blew her nose determinedly, lit another cigarette, and began to talk about her move south.

4

The Company, May & Baker (1937)

The typing pool was a completely new world for Mary. The noise stunned her. The clattering of so many keyboards was loud enough; the rustle of typing paper being fed between the rollers was familiar, but the constant clang of the carriage returns overwhelmed her. Shelves filled with reference books and medical journals divided the large room. She thought the whole place looked daunting, but it was, she saw immediately, a light airy space. Curled up on one of the bookcases oblivious to all the noise going on around it was a large black and white cat. She saw that any girl moving around and passing it stroked it absentmindedly, a caress that the cat completely ignored. She later learned it was the canteen cat and it was particularly partial to ginger biscuits but disdainful of any other kind of biscuits.

She had been given a map of the site layout so knew that behind the typing pool and the individual glass-caged offices of the senior staff was the factory itself. She had been given a brochure at her interview which stated that the plant employed nearly 4,000 people. She hid it well but felt overwhelmed and almost panic-stricken by the sheer scale of the place. Her previous workplaces were minute in comparison. It was all very intimidating.

Miss Brown, the typing pool supervisor, sensing Mary's consternation, smiled reassuringly at her.

"You'll get used to it – to the noise and the size of the place. In a day or two, you'll hardly notice the racket, and in a week, you'll feel at home. It's a friendly firm… in theory." She went on to explain, "All the typists work for any of the executives but actually they'll get used to a particular girl and always ask for her, and of course the girls get used to them. Most are very easy but one or two are a little prickly. Senior men have their own secretaries. I'll explain later."

She showed Mary to her desk and provided her with shorthand notebooks and pencils. "I'll leave you to settle in and later I'll take you round and introduce you. Tomorrow I'll find you some work."

The last thing she pressed into Mary's hand was the company's "red book", which contained the entire list of all products marketed under the company logo, listed under their pharmaceutical name, their code, and their product number. Opening it, Mary was filled with dismay. It might just as well have been in Japanese for all the sense it made.

The girl at the next desk, who introduced herself as Beatrice Shelby, reassured her, "Honestly, within a week you will begin to recognize all this. I know it looks like gobbledegook now but you will become so familiar with it. Everybody's been through it." One or two of the other girls looked up with curiosity at the newcomer and smiled or waved a casual but friendly hand.

"I'm Mary McCutchion."

"Scottish, I can tell; they'll call you Mac."

"Will they?" She was startled. "Why not my name, or even Miss McCutchion?"

"Everybody's called by their surname here – well, among the girls anyway, and some of the chaps too. Not heads of department of course or the senior bods, but the rest of us. It's sort of the firm's custom. I thought it odd at first, but now I quite like it."

She grinned cheerfully and Mary grinned back. She was engagingly friendly and Mary was only too pleased to be so warmly welcomed. Without further ado, Shelby introduced her to everyone as "Mac" and the name stuck. Mary never knew whether she would have been called Mac anyway or if it was her companion's introduction that was so calmly accepted.

May & Baker Ltd was a significant international company with a distinguished history. After the morning spent in a bewildering tour of the factory, Mary passed the afternoon deep in the red book. She thought with horror of transcribing the pharmaceutical terminology from shorthand to typescript. What the devil, she wondered, was an iodide and what did one use paraldehyde, phenobarbital, and hydroquinone for? Cocaine, she vaguely remembered, was used to numb the gum before some butcher of a dentist wrenched one's wisdom teeth out.

At lunch in the canteen, she met up with Shelby again. "How long have you worked here?" she asked. "How long did you take to get to grips with all this medical data?" She hoped she didn't look as anxious and overwhelmed as she felt.

"Look, stop worrying. Everybody knows you are new. They'll spell the words at first and in a week, if you do enough copy, you'll have them all off pat. Where are you living?"

"I've got digs at the moment, with a family friend in Hornchurch. I call her Aunt Kate." For some reason, Mary felt a bit defensive about her digs. As a modern career girl she felt she ought to be living somewhere independent and dashing.

Shelby sensed it and raised her eyebrows. "Sounds like a home from home!"

"Well yes, it's exactly what I *don't* want, but it will have to do for the moment." Actually, the digs were cheap and comfortable and Aunt Kate friendly, but Mary sensed that she would find it constraining very quickly. She hadn't come to London to be cosseted and mothered.

Two days later, she discovered that her new job was more specific than she had realized. Calling her into her office, Miss Brown explained that the secretary of one of the physicists was leaving and that he would need a replacement. "Miss Michaels is getting married in a couple of months and moving away so this will give you time…" she hesitated, "to learn his little ways!

We were impressed with your application letter. This is really why you have been taken on: eventually to hold a secretarial position. He's called Mr Choppin. He can be difficult, but he is very consistent."

Mary wasn't quite sure what that meant. "Do you mean consistently difficult?"

Miss Brown laughed. "No. I mean once you get used to him, you'll know where you are. He's regular. He doesn't chop and change. He's...well... consistent. Let me take you to meet him; beard the lion in his den." She gave a wry smile and ushered Mary into one of the glass cubicles behind the typing pool.

"Mr Choppin, this is Mac, who in due course will be taking over from Miss Michaels."

A handsome, slightly saturnine looking, dark-haired man aged, Mary guessed, about thirty, wearing horned-rim glasses, looked up from the dossier he was studying and stared at her. He was wreathed in blue cigarette smoke and Mary saw his ashtray was full. Without speaking, he pointed to the chair on the other side of his desk, and Mary sat. Nobody spoke. Miss Brown smiled brightly, nodded and left the room. The silence continued. Mary decided that she would not be the first to break it. After what seemed an interminable pause, he said, "Miss Mac?"

"No, Miss McCutchion, actually, but apparently I am to be known as Mac."

"Do you mind?"

She felt startled by the question. "No, not at all; it's quite fun to have a new name. Anyway, I don't think I have an option, do I?"

"No, I don't think you do," he said, with a sudden disarming grin that completely transformed his austere expression. There was another long pause, then he asked abruptly, "You are a long way from home. Why have you left Dunoon?"

"Dunoon's a small town. I thought there would be more opportunity in the south." *That's all he's going to get from me*, she thought.

He made no further comment, then after yet another long pause said, "I will dictate a letter and after that I'd like you to read it back. If I am happy, you can type it up." Something in her face made him say, "Don't worry about the technical and pharmaceutical terminology. I'll spell those. I don't like to be interrupted while I'm dictating so keep any questions until the end. I'll give you the address when I'm finished." She nodded, flipped open her notebook and waited. He got up and began to pace around.

"Dear Dr Anderson. Thank you for your swift response to my letter of 5th…" He stopped and Mary looked up. He was staring down at her notepad. "What the devil's that?" he asked.

"It's your letter, Mr Choppin!"

"But I can't read it!"

"You don't need to read it. I'm going to type it up and *then* you can read it."

"No, no, you don't understand. I know what shorthand looks like. This isn't shorthand! Is this a system of your own?"

"I did my commercial training, my stenographer's course, just after I left school in Buffalo in America. I was living there with my family. This is Gregg shorthand. The girls here do Pitman's, I think."

"But this is hopeless," he expostulated. "Nobody is going to be able to read your work!"

"Why would anybody need to read my notes? I'll type up my own work!"

"What happens if I ask you to type up another secretary's work? You won't be able to read their shorthand. Suppose you are off sick and I need your notes typed up? They won't be able to read them."

Mary thought to herself, *Yes, I can see why he is considered difficult.*

She drew in her breath and said as steadily as she could, "I've got used to Pitman's shorthand; I mean, I can make it out. But I really hope, Mr Choppin, that you won't ask me to type up another secretary's work, nor ask anyone else to type up mine. It's a risky business and considered very unprofessional." She saw by his face that the barb had met its mark, and added as a parting shot, "And actually, I don't remember ever being off sick."

He sat down at his desk and lit another cigarette. After a short pause, during which time he seemed lost in thought, he recommenced dictating. When she had finished scribbling he gave her the letter heading and verified the spellings of technical terms. She went back to her desk feeling exhausted but elated. When she had finished typing, she tapped on his door and handed the script to him. He took it, read it through, nodded, and then tore it in two, before tossing it into the wastepaper basket at the side of his desk.

She thought, *He's trying to unnerve me*, so she kept her face impassive.

"It's fine," he said. "Perfect. It was just a test. We'll start work tomorrow. Mike, that's Miss Michaels, will be back and you can learn the ropes."

"How did it go?" asked Miss Brown. Mary thought she looked apprehensive. "He's not everyone's cup of tea. I do hope you won't find him too difficult."

"I won't find him difficult at all," Mary replied with a dry laugh. "Challenging but really not difficult."

Interlude

I thought Frederick Choppin, her boss, sounded a nightmare: arrogant, domineering, and ruthlessly selfish. But she dismissed my opinion with a laugh. My mother had an amazing ability, sometimes, to see faults as nothing more than peccadillos, little character idiosyncrasies. This made me cross occasionally, when she glossed over quite serious defects or oddities of behaviour, saying, "Oh, you know what they are like; just ignore it!" I felt she was deluding herself, not seeing the real picture.

The fact was she had a soft spot for Choppin. Perhaps she was secretly proud of coping with somebody universally recognized as being awkward and difficult to work for, and she dismissed his often quite outrageous and petulant behaviour as if he were just a naughty schoolboy.

"I was packing for him once," she told me, "and found a whip in his case!"

"A whip? Do you mean a riding crop?"

"No, I don't think it was a riding crop. It could have been, though to my knowledge he never went riding. No, it definitely wasn't a riding crop. It was a whip; it would have hurt if you'd been struck with it."

"Mummy! Didn't you think it was deviant?"

"No," she replied with a grin. "I thought it was unsurprising and also I thought it was funny."

5

M&B and "the Wonder Drug" (1938)

*T*o Mary's surprise and disappointment, the excitement in the factory was muted when the synthesized product known by its batch name as M&B 693 was first marketed under its trade name Dagenan. The demand for it was huge and the workload for the staff increased steadily. Like penicillin, which was still in an experimental stage, sulphapyridine had been discovered almost by accident. Intense work began on research into its effects and on synthesizing other sulpha drugs, but the general atmosphere in the office was laconic, even low-key. She had hoped for great celebrations; if not champagne, a cake at least! But scientists, she discovered, were careful, even non-committal. The initial elation about the possibility of curing previously lethal infections was tempered with caution.

"Honestly, it's a major breakthrough and they are treating it like a really unimportant little episode," she complained to Choppin.

"What can happen in a Petri dish," he told her, "is often unexpected and may be extraordinary, but it's people who are going to be treated, and there may be side effects that will only show up later. We have to be wary of promising things that in the end may be less successful." Nevertheless, Mary thought it was thrilling, and she gave it two pages in her diary.

New pharmaceutical products were being produced regularly, but none touched the population so dramatically. Despite the scientific reserve, nothing could diminish the enthusiasm with which this remarkable new product was received by the public in general and the medical profession in particular. Streptococcal, staphylococcal, and pneumococcal infections were often fatal, so when M&B 693 and its fellow product M&B 760 proved to be a cure for killer diseases, they were hailed by the general public as wonder drugs.

"Furthermore," said Shelby with a sly grin, "that drug will keep other cheeky little cocks – or do I mean cocci – under control. It's effective, so Dr Forgan tells me, against gonorrhoea!" Dr Forgan was the senior venereologist.

"That's a very vulgar pun," said Choppin, overhearing as he passed, "but it's both clever and funny. Just don't let Dr Forgan hear it!"

Choppin kept Mary very busy indeed, as his correspondence was both national and international. When he wasn't in Dagenham he was overseas. She was disappointed that his numerous trips abroad, particularly to northern Europe, did not include her. She liked the idea of Sweden and Norway and, despite disquieting rumours about Germany, would certainly have gone there with enthusiasm. Alas, it never seemed to be on the cards, although with her usual cheeky self-confidence, she proposed it several times.

"I don't know why you don't take me with you, Mr Choppin. I could keep on top of the correspondence. Take notes for you at meetings. I wouldn't have so much to do when you got back." She was always frantically busy on his return. His expectations were very inflexible. It all had to be done to a particular standard and he made no concessions to overload, telling her that her shorthand, which was undecipherable to the other girls, made it difficult for her to offload work. "Which I warned you about," he pointed out tersely. She held to her position that typing up other people's work, or allowing others to do hers, was not professional, a matter she felt very strongly about. Occasionally, because of the huge amount of correspondence, he had to use another girl. He complained bitterly about it the whole time.

She found him standing beside her desk one afternoon. She recognized the scowl and the tight lips, and said calmly, "What's the matter, Mr Choppin?"

"What's the matter, Mac? I'll tell you what the matter is. This letter has three mistakes in it!" Mary took the document from his hand and glanced at it. "I'll do it for you," she said, "but I didn't type this."

He flushed with annoyance. "What? I remember dictating it to you."

"Mr Choppin, you are mistaken; you didn't dictate this to me. First, I would have remembered it, and secondly," she began to flip over the pages of her shorthand notebook, "it would be here. And it's not! Anyway, it's not my typing."

"Whatever do you mean? Typing is typing; it's not a handwritten letter. It's produced by a machine!"

She saw the scepticism on his face and, without speaking, left her own desk and began to make her way down the room to others. With a nod to her colleagues, she picked up several type-written letters from various out-trays. Back at her own desk, with Choppin standing fuming beside it, she shuffled the scripts and then laid them face down in front of him. "Please pick one up," she said. The other secretaries from whose trays she had taken the scripts began to draw closer. Choppin picked one up and held it out.

"That's mine," said Shelby. Mary looked at Choppin and nodded her chin towards the pile. He picked up another.

"Mine," said Marshall. "I've got a very heavy strike."

He picked up a third.

"Yes, I'm afraid that's me. Good heavens! I hope it's OK!" Dalton, a shy but diligent girl, looked horrified at the possibility of being found wanting.

At the fourth Mary said, "That one's mine!"

Choppin stood for a moment with his head down. Mary expected an outburst: he hated to be challenged. But, with his often unexpected charm, he said, "I apologize, ladies. I now know that any secretary worth her salt recognizes her own typing." Turning to Mary and grinning at her, he said, "Would you please be kind enough to retype this letter for me, Mac? I accept it's not yours."

"Of course, Mr Choppin." She decided, in the interests of harmony, not to pursue the provenance of the badly typed letter. He really was infuriating, she thought, cross as a bear and intimidating, and then completely charming. Because of this charm, she knew she was sometimes the object of envy in having, others believed, such a delightful boss. Nothing could have been further from the truth. He was exacting, and irascible. All the charming smiles in the world didn't make him easy to work for. Despite that, and because she liked a challenge, she enjoyed working with him. She knew he was more than satisfied with her, though praise was in short supply. Sometimes he asked her to do things clearly outside the remit of any secretary.

"If you go up to the West End on Saturday, will you go into every chemist you pass, and buy this brand of toothpaste – and only this one." He passed her a piece of paper with the name of a well-known make on it. He looked at her very seriously. "Then," he continued, "please make a note of how many chemists ask you to sign the Poison Register. They all should: it's got arsenic in it!"

"Honestly," Mary told Shelby, "I feel as if I am working undercover for the Secret Service."

"Perhaps you are! Did he say who he was going to report his findings to?"

Mary never learned the outcome of her odd mission. What she did discover was that of the seven or eight outlets she visited, only two asked her to sign the poison book.

Choppin was not alone in finding Mary competent and charming. She became, unexpectedly, the object of attention from Dr Maxwell, the managing director, who never failed to stop for a brief chat every time he passed through the office.

Initially, she was disconcerted by his attention and cross when she was teased by the others about what was clearly a partiality. Fortunately, as he was very nearly old enough to be her father, she acquitted him of any motive other than friendliness. It didn't stop some spiteful gossip but she rode it well, shrugging it off. Personally she thought he was delightful and responded cheerfully to his questions.

"How are you settling in, Mac? I hope Mr Choppin is not proving too difficult. I know how irascible he can be." Dr Maxwell was very fond of Scotland, he told her, and he and his French wife often holidayed in Argyll. This, she realized, was an excuse for him to chat about the delights of sailing in Tighnabruaich or attending the Cowal Highland Games held every year in Dunoon.

"I promise you, if he makes a pass at me, I'll let you know," she told Shelby and Fraser, another office friend. Gossip was meat and drink to any large company and what was topical one day was passé the next, so after a time "Dr Maxwell's little pet" became yesterday's news.

There were other things to preoccupy May & Baker in 1938. The disquieting news from Germany and the political unrest elsewhere in Europe had repercussions for the company. Many of the base products came from abroad, and anxiety about sourcing essential manufacturing material was high.

Mary had her own upheavals. She didn't stay long in digs with Aunt Kate. Coming home about 11 p.m. one night, after a pleasant evening in the cinema with friends, she found the good lady sitting on the stairs in her dressing gown.

"Oh, Maisie, I've been so worried about you. It's gone eleven! What would I say to your dear mother if anything happened to you?"

It took over half an hour and two mugs of cocoa to calm her. This was exactly, Mary thought crossly, what she had escaped from at home. She knew it was time to move on. She found herself a charming, two-bedroom, first-floor flat to rent in

Upminster, within easy travelling distance of Dagenham. It was a very pleasant area, almost countryside, with tree-lined streets and a large park. From her bedroom she could see the sails of Upminster Windmill.

Several of her colleagues, among others Shelby and Fraser, came to help her move in. She had little furniture, but between them, with a great deal of laughter and ingenuity, they made cupboards and storage spaces from the wooden fruit boxes that the traders gave away. Mary eventually covered them with pretty material bought from a market stall. She acquired a three-piece suite on the "never-never" and Fraser's parents gave her a bed they wanted to get rid of, which she accepted cheerfully and gratefully. She spent what she thought was an inordinate amount of money on a new divan bed for the second bedroom, and a carpet for the sitting-room made by a firm in Glasgow as a nod to her Scottishness. Her girlfriends, with a mixture of cajolery and flirtatious persuasion, roped in what they called "some muscle". Two pleasant young men, Shayler and Kettlewood, the latter known as "K", heaved the furniture upstairs. In the evening, dusty, hot, and sweaty but cheerfully satisfied, they all went to the Railway Hotel in Dagenham for beer and sandwiches. This was a favourite lunchtime haunt for the staff at May & Baker as an occasional change from the canteen.

Leaning on the bar was a young man Mary had seen in the office among the reps. He greeted everybody with easy familiarity and came to join them. He was not tall, rather thick-set and swarthy, with a head of black hair, very dark eyes, and a moustache. Mary thought he had a vaguely Spanish look about him; Fraser thought he looked like a gypsy but couldn't deny his attractiveness. His name was Colin MacCallum-Stewart. He had a lovely smile and a friendly open manner. The evening passed pleasantly and before it broke up, this new acquaintance invited Mary to the cinema the following Saturday.

Interlude

As this was someone who figured significantly in my life, I wanted to ask more about the beginning of her relationship with my father. "So what did you think of him? I mean, how did he strike you?"

She smiled, a small, secretive little smile. "Well," she said, "he was not handsome in the strict sense of the word but he had immense sex appeal. There was something about him. He liked women. He enjoyed their company. He wasn't flirtatious; it was deeper than that."

I waited expectantly.

"He was always very gallant; he could really charm women." Then she added mischievously, "I'm sure they were all wondering what he was like in bed! I discovered later he was wonderful."

I could only smile at her honesty, and as their relationship had gone through some very hard times I was glad that their conjugal life together had known some high spots too.

6

Gathering Clouds and War (1938–39)

*C*olin became a regular member of Mary's friendship group. At the weekends many of them would go up to town, sometimes to the West End to see a show, and sit happily in the "gods" – the upper circle. The view gave a distinctly foreshortened perspective of the stage, and the actors looked about two foot tall. But that high up, the acoustics were the best in the theatre. At least that was what they told each other. Occasionally on Sundays, just for fun and to search for bargains, they went to Petticoat Lane in the East End, an easy ride on the train. Happy and contented in her new home with a pleasant circle of friends, Mary really felt she had "arrived".

It was tacitly accepted by everybody that Colin was her boyfriend, and they were viewed as a couple. If they went to the cinema or the theatre he sat beside her, and on the bus or train, they would save a seat for each other. Without being in love, she began to think of him with deep affection.

At New Year and again at Easter she went home to Scotland to stay with her parents and take up old friendships. She had a very enjoyable time despite the pressure her parents' placed on her to return home. At the Argyll Hotel where she had taken them for afternoon tea, she tried to explain.

"My home is London now. I've got a good job, a flat, and friends." Her father was always more insistent, pointing out with enthusiasm what he saw as the advantages that Dunoon had to offer over Dagenham. Now that she'd made her break for freedom and experienced the wider world, he reasoned, she would be happy to return home. But it was the pain on her mother's face that moved her most. She took her hands and gently removed the hanky that she was twisting between her fingers.

"Mama, isn't it much better that I come home like this, every few months, and we have a lovely time together? We can chat and laugh, catch up, and really get on. If I were back here permanently, I would be restless and disappointed, because Dunoon, lovely as it is, has so little to offer me. Worse, I would be so bad-tempered. You must see that!" Michael's shadow hung over the conversation, an unspoken reason for her new life elsewhere.

Every holiday there was always one episode like that, and rather than issuing her parents with an ultimatum such as, "Either you stop trying to persuade me or I won't come home", she learned to cope by laughing it off. She continued her twice-yearly visits, and one year her mother braved the journey south. Mary's friends made a great fuss of her. Colin had gone on holiday to visit his father, so mother and boyfriend didn't meet, which Mary found something of a relief. She'd had quite enough of parents and boyfriends.

In the early winter of 1939 Mr Choppin went to India on the firm's business and Mary found herself at a loose end. He had left work for her but not enough to keep her fully occupied. She re-organized his filing cabinets and volunteered to sort out the archive room. After a week, she confessed herself beaten, not only by the sheer volume of the documents but by the dust and filth of the area. She never did discover where all the sooty debris that coated all the files came from. It took an hour to wash it all out of her hair, even if she wore a turban. She filled in for other staff absences on an ad hoc basis but became bored because she didn't have enough to do. Her diary was filled with irritable comments about her colleagues, her workplace and the weather. It was no fun at all to read by the end of the week.

The German annexation of the Sudetenland, followed by what was talked of as the rape of Czechoslovakia, had left nobody with any illusions about German territorial ambitions. A terrible anxiety settled over the country, a heavy oppressive weight. Fraser, who had family in Nuremberg, had returned from a visit with dreadful stories of overt anti-Semitism. She also had photos of the militaristic rallies that she had the good luck or misfortune, depending on your views, to attend, and these were even more alarming. Everybody, Fraser told Mary, except the most ardent appeasers, knew the Munich Agreement wasn't worth the paper it was written on.

Colin turned up at Mary's flat one spring evening after work. She wasn't expecting him, but, alarmed by the expression on his face, brought him in. Sitting on her little sofa, he took her hands and gave her his news. She realized afterwards that all over Britain similar scenarios were taking place. Colin said quietly, "The reservists are being called up and shortly I imagine it will be any able-bodied man over twenty. It really looks like war; it's inevitable I think. I don't know any definite date for my own call-up but it will be soon. I'll try and give you some warning. Don't be too anxious."

She was stricken by his news. It was not completely unexpected. She knew he had been in the army after leaving school. But she burst into tears and threw her arms around him. He tried unsuccessfully to comfort her but eventually, trying to be sensible, she dried her tears, blew her nose and said crossly, "Yes, yes, I know; it'll all be over by Christmas! Where have we heard *that* before?"

He laughed and then produced a hip flask, saying, "I thought you might need this." So they sat sipping brandy until, rather tipsy, they fell into bed together. Before he left, he said, "Will you knit me a balaclava?" She promised he would have the best balaclava ever and duly presented it to him a week later. He was gone the following day.

In the office over the next few months there was considerable restlessness, and by late August other men were disappearing. K went into the Pioneers, Woodford into the Engineers.

Fielding, who used to call Choppin "Machiavelli" and teased Mary, calling her "Becky Sharp", went into Intelligence – information which caused general hilarity and ribald laughter. This delightfully friendly young man, charming though he was, was considered dim beyond belief.

"You have to explain the simplest jokes to him," said Marshall, another of Mary's particular friends. "God help the country if he's in Intelligence."

The firm recruited others to fill the gaps of those who left. The place didn't seem quite the same, and Mary was bored beyond belief. She greeted Choppin's return with unalloyed pleasure. He brought back presents for several of his friends and a pair of ebony bookends shaped as elephants for her, with a silver plaque engraved "To Mac with my most grateful thanks". She was very touched.

Distressingly she had no news from Colin. He had been gone nearly four months. She decided not to go to Dunoon for her summer break in case he should turn up unexpectedly, using as an excuse that she wanted to paint the flat. She should have realized the consequences of this decision. Arriving home from work on 31 August, she found her mother sitting on the doorstep.

"I could hardly turn her away, could I?" she told Miss Brown next morning. "But I can tell you I wasn't very pleased. What am I going to do with her? If I can square it with Mr Choppin, can I take a couple of days' leave to give me time to persuade her to go home?"

On 3 September, Mary, along with most of the country, listened to the declaration of war, unsurprised but nevertheless horrified and depressed. Her mother thereupon stalwartly refused to return to Scotland unless Mary accompanied her.

"This is ridiculous, Mama. I've got a job and a flat here; of course I'm not going back with you!"

"I'll talk to her," volunteered Choppin.

He was as good as his word: he took her out to lunch at Simpsons and bought her a beautiful handbag that she admired from Swan and Edgar, but nevertheless he had to confess himself beaten. She was determined to stay until she could persuade her daughter to return to Dunoon. He didn't mind about the cost – he told Mary when she tried to reimburse him – but he was astonished that he, who considered himself the most persuasive of men, had failed at what he thought would be a simple task.

Finally, Mary's father put an end to the stand off. The telegram was authoritative and definitive: "Jane – (stop) – Come home immediately – (stop) – I need you here – (stop) –". She bowed to the voice of her husband and caught the night sleeper to Glasgow.

7

Marriage

The complete absence of any aggressive activity on the part of the Germans on British home territory in the immediate aftermath of the declaration of war was unnerving.

"I thought we would be bombed straight away," said Fraser. "My mother's been packing the china and stocking up on candles." This was premature, but in the long run quite sensible. Other significant practical steps were taken. The company necessarily detached itself by mutual agreement from its French partners and there was consequently some difficulty in acquiring, among other things, ampoules for pharmaceutical products. Indeed, the whole question of supplies from mainland Europe was a major issue. Other essential materials were sourced from the USA and from a UK manufacturing plant in Leek, Staffordshire, and were developed to provide some base products.

The roof of the factory was given a coat of camouflage paint which the maintenance department said wouldn't fool anybody and those were prescient words. Air-raid shelters were dug, gas masks issued, and the prospect of general rationing was mooted. Christmas 1939 came and went, and the initial fear about the possibility of a German invasion abated.

Sitting at her typewriter one morning, engrossed in her work, Mary felt a slight movement behind her and turned round to find Colin grinning down at her. She gave a great shout of pleasure and, jumping to her feet, threw her arms about him. He was in uniform but round his cap band there was a white stripe.

"Oh, Colin, my darling," she said. "Wherever have you come from?"

"Actually I've come from Sandhurst," he said, pointing to the white band. "I was in France in Brest, but now I've been granted a commission. In addition, I have seniority because of my previous service. I'm still in training at the moment but in three months you will be looking at Lieutenant MacCallum-Stewart. I still have the balaclava," he added. Then picking her up he swung her round and the whole area burst into spontaneous clapping.

They settled back into their routine, he coming to Upminster when he was off duty and she feeling increasingly happy and at ease in his company. He could be extraordinarily tender and thoughtful, making her tea, helping with the washing up, even running the sweeper over the carpets; activities she could never remember either her father or her two brothers ever undertaking. She loved his sense of humour and found him intelligent and articulate. There was something very seductive, she decided, about a man who could make her laugh. She took a small snapshot of him with her Box Brownie camera and pasted it into her diary. He seemed very pleased but she wouldn't let him read the entry.

He was also delighted to help by putting up shelves and mowing the small lawn of the communal garden. With his help, the flat was finally painted. On another occasion, he arrived with some old carpeting to put into the air-raid shelter. He also purloined three camp beds; she didn't ask from where. "You're going to need these!" he told her. The relief she felt at his safe reappearance was reinforced by the grim news from across the Channel and she thanked God he was taking no part in that.

With the invasion of Belgium and Holland the writing was on the wall for France, and with the capture of Paris, the capitulation of the French government was inevitable. The British Expeditionary Force together with the Belgian and French military, which had expected at least to hold back the advancing Germans, were completely overwhelmed. By the end of May, the British were fighting for their lives, with their backs to the sea, on the beaches at Dunkirk.

Coming into work one day, Mary found Miss Brown with some of the girls gathered round her, a few in tears.

A sudden wave of nausea swept over her. "Oh, God! Whatever's happened?"

Shelby put her arm round her and for one appalling moment she thought "Colin!", until she remembered he was safe in Aldershot.

"It's Fielding; his mother phoned Dr Maxwell this morning. He's been killed. We all feel bad because of how we used to laugh at him and think how useless he'd be in Intelligence."

It was a very sober day. This news seemed a symbolic end to the "phoney war" and for Mary it came with terrifying suddenness. Walking home across Upminster Park a few days later, she was shocked into panic by a sudden outburst of gunfire. She didn't know it at the time but it could well have been the first dogfight of the Battle of Britain. Above her head in a cloudless sky, planes were dodging and weaving, with puffs of smoke like cotton wool bursting around them. The noise of the aircraft and the intermittent machine-gun fire filled the air. Even the earth seemed to tremble. The noise was alarming, but it was the realization of what was happening that terrified her.

"Lie down, lie down!" She saw soldiers shouting at her from the path. "Don't look up, don't look up!" She threw herself to the ground with a pounding heart, breathless with fear. It was the first time she had ever heard gunfire; it would not be the last. She was still trembling when she arrived back at her cosy reassuring little flat. She could not have been more frightened, she told Colin later, if she had seen a German soldier running towards her with a bayonet in his hand.

Colin received his commission into the Royal Berkshire Regiment in the middle of June, and was posted to Brock Barracks in Reading. Walking home with her from the cinema one evening on a weekend's leave, he said abruptly, "You know, Mac, I'm terribly fond of you. I think we ought to get married."

"Oh, Colin!" She looked at him with tenderness and sighed.

"No, no, listen! I'm going to be posted somewhere soon. The war is really upon us now. I could be killed or wounded, and I would really like to think I was living for something, for somebody. We get on really well and I'm not a bad chap; don't you like the idea of having an officer for a husband?" He said this with a deprecating laugh but she knew he was serious. "We can get married by special licence."

It all seemed reasonable. She *was* very fond of him. It *was* wartime. So, after a moment, smiling, she replied, "Yes, please," and he grinned and whooped like a schoolboy.

In the office she said she was being married a week Saturday and issued a general invitation. In Hornchurch, she bought a pretty, powder blue linen suit with a dashing hat. Colin told her afterwards that it reminded him of a saucepan lid. She found a delightful pair of navy suede shoes and a matching handbag. They ordered a barrel of beer and sandwiches and booked the private function room at the Railway Hotel. Fraser and Shelby were her witnesses and stood as unofficial bridesmaids. Sugar rationing had been introduced in January 1940 but several of her friends in the office contributed their ration in lieu of a wedding present. A baker in Dagenham made her an iced cake, the last from his shop until the end of the war.

Mary, escorted by her two friends, arrived at Romford Registry Office in good time. At 12:15 p.m., there was no sign of the bridegroom and at 12:25 p.m., although she was not worried, she was annoyed. The wedding was booked for 12:30 p.m. He erupted into the waiting room, immaculate in his uniform but breathless and laughing. His train had been delayed and, as he didn't know where the Registry Office was situated, had leapt into a taxi outside the station. Shouting the required destination, he said, "Quick as you can, I'm late!" The taxi driver drove about a hundred yards up the street, turned left and pulled up outside the Registry Office. Colin could have walked it in about a minute.

"Have this one on me!" said the taxi driver grinning. "Good luck, mate, and I hope she doesn't give you a hard time."

The 3rd August was a glorious summer day. The pub had a pleasant garden and they were able to move from the stiff formality of the function room out onto the lawn. It was a relaxed and happy occasion. Sitting on the grass and surrounded by friends, her new husband's arms around her, Mary found it was almost possible to forget the war. There were no dogfights overhead to mar such an idyllic day. In the evening they went, just the two of them, to the cinema to see *Rebecca*, a prosaic but pleasant, easy thing to do. The next night they took the sleeper to Glasgow, then the train to Gourock and the ferry to Dunoon, so that her new husband could meet her parents. It passed off amicably, no fuss or reproaches. Both parents, astonishingly, seemed to accept the *fait accompli* with equanimity. She wondered briefly if they would have accepted Michael in the end if she had gone ahead and faced them down.

Their Scottish honeymoon passed swiftly, and immediately on their return to Upminster, Colin received his posting. He stood in the flat with the MOD communication in his hand, and announced, "It's as I expected; it's West Africa. The Royal West African Frontier Force wants me as a training officer. I get promotion too! I arrive as Captain MacCallum-Stewart." He was so delighted that Mary hid her dismay; his departure was not unexpected after all.

She felt desperately lonely after he'd gone and not a little sorry for herself: no boss and no husband. She didn't feel at all married, particularly as her soubriquet "Mac" didn't change.

"Nobody's going to call you 'MacCallum-Stewart'," laughed Miss Brown.

"What about 'Stewart'?" Mary proposed hopefully, but despite several hints nobody took her up on it, so Mac she remained.

The person who showed the most disapproval when he learned about her marriage was Mr Choppin. He had been recalled to India to deal with a serious health issue. The manager of the branch was gravely ill and not expected to live.

Mary could tell from the tone of the letter she received that he was more than a little put out by her news, although he sent her a silver tea service as a wedding present.

"Miserable old thing," commented Shelby. "He just doesn't want to share you!" Mary knew this was true. He was very possessive. On one notable occasion he even expressed resentment when Dr Maxwell had borrowed her for a day to help his secretary classify some pharmaceutical documentation.

"He says he'll have you for his secretary if Madison leaves and furthermore he won't give you back," Choppin told her sourly.

"Fear not, Mr Choppin," Mary reassured him smiling. "I shall never desert Mr Micawber." She knew by his frown that he didn't recognize the quotation and that he would be annoyed by that, so she took pity on him: "Charles Dickens. *David Copperfield*. It's what Mrs Micawber says every time her husband is incarcerated in the debtors' prison."

"Oh, Mac!" he laughed, as he disappeared back into his office.

The battle for mastery of the air continued unabated all during that long hot summer. There was no relief from the German aggression. When Britain began to gain ascendancy over the Luftwaffe, the Blitz dominated everybody's life. At night Mary began to loathe the stuffy confines of the air-raid shelter. Dagenham might well have been some distance from

London, but it was an industrial centre on the Thames with a large Ford car factory, May & Baker, and other plant. It had a dock, a mainline railway, and the Underground. Hornchurch aerodrome was close by. Every night, from the dubious security of the shelter in the garden, Mary and her neighbours, huddling in the confines of their garden bunker, heard the German bombers coming in, following the treacherous silver ribbon of the river into the heartland of the city. Their sleep was minimal but Colin's camp beds at least allowed horizontal rest. The "crump-crump" of the bombardment and the rattle of anti-aircraft fire broke the night.

One night a bomb fell in the street outside the flat, blowing in every pane of glass. Mary told Colin in a letter that the walls of the shelter seemed to expand and contract. It was her first experience of a blast, but nobody was hurt. The "all clear" at daybreak brought freedom from the claustrophobic atmosphere of the shelter but no morning freshness. Mary, along with everybody else, felt permanently tired. Even a wash or sometimes a quick bath before work did not alleviate the all-encompassing exhaustion. It occurred to her that, compared to West Africa, Dagenham and even Upminster (where Mary's flat was) were having a rough time.

"He's the soldier," she told Miss Brown, who had enquired pleasantly about Colin, "but I'm the one at war."

The maintenance department of May & Baker were correct in their assessment of the efficacy of the camouflage paint on the roof of the factory. In September and October the shipping office and export sales department were hit, but fortunately injuries were relatively minor. Mary never saw the canteen cat again. Nobody knew if it had been killed or whether it had just decided to move to a quieter, less dangerous area.

Mary went home at Christmas. It was a protracted journey with frequent stops. She thought Glasgow had escaped lightly and Dunoon seemed another world.

Interlude

"Did you love him? Colin, my father, I mean? It sounds a curiously lightweight sort of commitment."

I really wanted to know about my parents' relationship. Once again we were ensconced in her little sitting room, she wreathed in cigarette smoke, me with my whisky. I was beginning to enjoy this intimacy.

"It was all a bit sudden, wasn't it, and somehow passionless?"

She got up and went to her chest of drawers, producing from it one of her diaries and a handful of photos I had never seen. Her black and white wedding photo showed a bashful looking young woman in an ill-fitting suit wearing an extraordinary flat hat perched precariously on the side of her head. Her expression was sweet. Beside her, Colin smiled confidently at the camera, very smart in his No. 2 uniform, his Sam Browne belt gleaming and the three pips on his epaulettes showing his captain's rank.

"Well," she said tersely, "I don't know about passionless. It was hasty but it was wartime; nobody knew if they'd see another day. Nobody thought long-term; nobody dared to. People grabbed life by the throat. In the long run, of course, we weren't very compatible, but at the time..." Her voice trailed off. "Well," she brightened up, "we had two lovely children after all, so not a totally bad choice." Then she smiled at me and lit another cigarette.

I didn't pursue it. She told me another time they had had many happy times, that he was fun, dynamic, and hardworking, but the truth was they were temperamentally quite unsuited, and their life together had as many dark times as it had bright.

8

The Departure

FEBRUARY **1941**

$\mathcal{D}$r Maxwell sat with her letter in front of him. He was silent for a long moment. Then, clearing his throat, he said, "My dear Mac. My dear Miss McCutchion... no, that's wrong too." He started again: "My dear Mrs Stewart, surely you don't mean to leave us?"

"Dr Maxwell, my husband is away, my boss is away, I have no work. I hate having idle hands and the services are very keen for volunteers. I could be much more usefully employed in another capacity, working directly for the war effort." She knew this was over-dramatic but felt the need to emphasize her restless dissatisfaction. He would talk her out of it otherwise, she thought.

"I would much prefer to stay here but there is nothing for me to do. The work that Mr Choppin sends keeps me occupied for a day at the most."

He sat frowning down at his desk for a moment then he looked up and stared directly at her. "I'm going to ask you something and I want you to think very carefully before you reply." He got up and began to pace around, moving piles of papers from his desk to the top of his filing cabinet, and then shifting them back again. She recognized this displacement activity, but was nevertheless startled by what followed.

"Would you like to go to India? Mr Choppin would be delighted and you wouldn't lack for work there, I can assure you!" He seemed to feel, if the smile on his face was anything to go by, that he had solved her problem.

She felt a great rush of excitement and could only gasp, "Dr Maxwell, if you want me to go to India, I will go to India."

She barely heard the rest. Lightheaded and bewildered, she came out of his office with a piece of paper covered in instructions. Within the next week, she was inoculated and issued with a passport. This later acquisition had been difficult. At the passport office, she received a blank refusal and the usual surly, "Don't you know there's a war on?" Her explanation that she worked for a famous pharmaceutical company and her presence in India was essential for the maintenance of their international market was met with some scepticism, but she argued her case determinedly. Actually, she told Shelby, she didn't give a fig for the international market, but she got her passport. Her friend was beside herself with excitement when Mary offered her the flat for the nine to eighteen months that Dr Maxwell told her she might be away. She was not surprised by the reaction that came when the news of her departure and the destination became known in the office. Snide remarks about Dr Maxwell's little pet began to resurface, and one of the senior secretaries expressed bitter resentment to Mary's face, that Mary had been chosen over her.

"But you don't like Mr Choppin," Mary told her. "You've never made any secret of that!" Actually, what she really wanted to say was, "He can't stand *you*! He'd send you back. He wouldn't even let you off the ship."

"Don't bother about it," Fraser reassured her. "They're just jealous."

In some ways, Mary was amused by the situation, particularly as there would have been more cause for jealousy had her envious companions known to what extent Dr Maxwell had taken her under his wing and supervised all the arrangements personally. She was given thirty pounds (a considerable sum in 1940) to buy suitable clothes for the tropics and, arriving at work one morning, was collared by Tom Shayler, who told her that she was to accompany Dr Maxwell up to town to buy her luggage. She was pleased that she'd got her new cream coat on, a present from Colin. She thought of his delight had he known that she was being kitted out at the company's expense.

In the travel department of Harrods, under her boss's avuncular eye (she hoped), she bought a cabin trunk and two suitcases. She thought her shopping was finished, but then Dr Maxwell said, "Just a moment." Under the pretext of choosing something for his wife, he selected a beautiful dressing case. It was calfskin, exquisitely lined with black moiré silk. The interior was frilled and pleated. The tray was filled with brushes of silver and green enamel, and under the tray were bottles to hold perfume and toilet water, together with a manicure set. Mary thought she had never seen anything so beautiful. Dr Maxwell presented it to her solemnly over lunch and her protests were brushed aside. She was well aware that this was not the usual sort of leaving present to a junior member of a company from a managing director, but as there seemed no way of refusing it, she accepted it with unreserved pleasure.

Farewells in the office were muted: "We will miss you a great deal." Miss Brown's was probably the most direct: "I hope you'll be back soon!" Others said goodbye pleasantly. Mary comforted herself by remembering that no great fuss had been made over the departure of the men who had been called up, nor over the girls who left to work elsewhere. Shelby and Fraser took her to lunch at the Railway Hotel and she spent her last night in the flat packing and writing to Colin and her parents.

On 9 March, she travelled up to Liverpool. She had been booked into the Adelphi Hotel. She was cheered to be met by the local May & Baker manager and together they spent the forty-eight hours she had before embarking on the ship looking around the city. Work on the huge Anglican cathedral, which was at that time under construction, had been halted for the duration of the war. Mary thought it extraordinarily ugly, but had to be impressed by its size. She decided she liked Liverpool. It had a buzzing atmosphere and she found the people friendly, although the Scouse accent was almost as incomprehensible to her as her own Scottish brogue was to them.

The hotel was very grand but, despite the elegance of her room, Mary slept badly for her two-night stay – probably from excitement, she thought. On the morning of her departure her company colleague arrived with a huge bouquet of flowers and a bottle of champagne. She didn't have the heart to tell him that she detested champagne, reflecting that others would enjoy it, so she thanked him with enthusiasm. He drove her down to the docks in good time and saw her aboard her ship and into the small but adequate cabin. After he'd gone, she unpacked and then went up onto the deck to watch the vessel cast off its lines and manoeuvre away from the dock. Two other passenger ships left at about the same time and the little fleet sailed out in convoy, accompanied by two naval frigates.

The ship SS *Britannia* was an Anchor Line vessel with a mainly Goan crew. The passengers were a mixture of civilians, army personnel, and other British servicemen. The ship, without being luxurious, was comfortable and had a charming 1930s elegance about it. Falling asleep that first night in her upper bunk, Mary determined to enjoy herself and, in the beginning, she did just that.

Interlude

The story of the beautiful dressing case amused me. Dr Maxwell's partiality for my mother did not sound in the least avuncular, and I was not at all surprised that she should be the object of catty remarks and jealous gossip, even if the office didn't know about the present. I thought her astonishingly naïve about the whole thing. "You must have known he was... well, coming on to you."

She declared heatedly that my remark bordered on the prurient. "He was old enough to be my father," she said sternly, then added, "Well, almost."

I thought her whole relationship with Dr Maxwell was odd. It seemed to me that he took a personal interest in her. How could she fail to see how inappropriate his gift to her was? I thought it another example of her ability to ignore the obvious in relationships. Later, I thought she knew only too well what was going on, but yet enjoyed it.

9

The Ship

*T*here were advantages, she thought, to having the upper bunk, if it meant she could assess the day without leaving her bed. Lifting the blackout curtain over the porthole, she could peer out at both sea and sky. She would have preferred the haughty, unfriendly QA (an army nurse from the Queen Alexandra's Royal Army Nursing Corps) who shared her cabin to have asked her directly if she would be willing to change places, rather than go to the purser. He had summoned her politely but was, poor man, quite pink with embarrassment due to the nature of his request.

"It's your allocated place – the bunk you were given when you booked, Mrs Stewart; here it is." He showed her the manifest and pointed out her name. "There you are: Mrs Mary Stewart, Cabin 24, lower bunk; and if you say no, that'll be that."

"Yes, of course she can have the lower bunk, but why on earth didn't she ask me directly, rather than make this all so formal?"

"It's probably the way they do things in the army. This is really kind of you. I am most grateful." The look of relief on his face made Mary think that the QA had been harder to deal with.

Billy, the friendly Goan steward, brought her tea every morning and she would take it from him and ask about the weather while she propped herself up on her elbow and took sips of tea.

There was a sort of grunt from the bunk below as the occupant took her tea from the steward. There was no "thank you", but Mary wasn't surprised. *She* hadn't been thanked either, for giving up the lower bunk. She knew that the nurse disapproved of her friendly morning exchanges with Billy, *fraternizing with the other ranks*, perhaps, so she deliberately prolonged the chats and the pleasantries, particularly if her cabin mate was still in bed. Mary had as little to do with her as possible. She felt proud at having overcome the initial resentment generated by the disproportionate space that the nurse had taken in the wardrobe. "My uniforms really do need to hang," she had announced, appropriating the majority of the coat hangers. Mary considered her own clothes quite as worthy of coat hangers, but felt it would have been demeaning to have entered into such a petty insistence on her rights.

"Poor thing. The other nurses don't like her, you know," Mrs Harrison, one of the two Methodist missionaries on board, told her one morning at breakfast. She spoke with easy sympathy. These pleasant women had kindly invited Mary to join them at their table when they realized she was travelling alone. "You can tell by their faces. She must be lonely. I think she has quite a high rank, major or lieutenant colonel." Mary actually didn't consider major or lieutenant colonel a particularly high rank and thought it certainly didn't justify the self-importance of the nurse in question, but didn't say so.

Mrs Harrison's companion, Miss Phelps, interjected to change the subject. She was a pale statuesque redhead who, despite being a nurse, didn't look nearly robust enough for the rigours of the Indian climate that she would face when she arrived in Bombay. She spoke with a nervous gasp, as if amazed at her own temerity.

"Mrs Stewart, I believe you are in charge of finding players for the darts match. It's on the notice-board."

Mary replied, "Yes I am, for my sins. The purser collared me yesterday. I know nothing about darts but he assures me I don't have to play, just find about a dozen people to make up teams. It's next week, so I've got a bit of time." Miss Phelps blushed, an all-enveloping colouration from her face to the slender column of her neck, and even to the modest décolletage revealed by the open collar of her blouse. When she blushed, Mary saw it went all the way down; Mary imagined even her toes turning pink.

"You see, I have four brothers. They taught me to play and very cross they were too when I regularly beat them. It's in the eye and the wrist, you know." She blushed even more fiercely, clearly ashamed of her boldness. "I hope you don't think I am being boastful; I mean I'm not a fantastically good player but… ." Her voice trailed off.

"Miss Phelps," said Mary firmly, "you are a godsend. Does this mean you are volunteering? If so, would you like to help me drum up some more competitors?"

The girl hesitated. "I just need to ask: there's no gambling involved, is there?" Mary remembered the nonconformists' view about gambling, smoking, and alcoholic drinks and rushed to reassure her.

"Heavens, no. At least I don't think so, but we can find out. We'll ask the purser; he knows everything."

There was a little area off the lounge, pretentiously called "the library" on the strength of its eclectic collection of books. These included a 1910 *Encyclopaedia Britannica*, bound copies of the *London Illustrated News*, and a battered copy of *Mrs Beeton's Book of Household Management*. Disconcertingly, there was also an alarming tome entitled *The Diagnosis and Treatment of Tropical Parasites* with gruesome illustrations. Mary studied it with careful fascination. A motley selection of tired, dog-eared romances and thrillers completed the selection, left behind – if the *ex-libris* dedications were any indication – by previous passengers.

It was here, every morning, that she found a comfortable armchair in which to curl up and write her diary. She was shy about revealing this activity, feeling that writing a diary was an old-fashioned thing to do. She had done it since she was a girl. Mary was methodical and liked keeping a record of her activities, so it seemed a sensible thing to do. It also allowed her to make personal comments and observations, both complimentary and critical, about anything and indeed anybody. The QA had a whole page to herself.

Every Saturday evening, with cosy self-indulgence, she found time to read her personal account of the week. Occasionally she was startled by what she recognized as a snide or even malicious comment, and would then annotate it "Didn't really mean this" or "Perhaps I misunderstood". Sometimes she re-annotated the annotations: "Yes I did!" or "OH NO!" or "Should think about this". Her diary, she believed, was both an observation of her environment and a confirmation of her place in it. It was Mary Stewart's declaration of herself.

She knew herself to be a pretty woman: small, dark-haired, with pale delicate skin, and slender ankles. The latter gave her immense personal satisfaction, although, generally speaking, despite her pride in her appearance, she was without vanity. Myopic, she had worn glasses since she was twelve but had never found this a detriment to her general appeal or attractiveness. An intelligent quick-witted girl with a good analytical mind, she was also impulsive, fun-loving, and gregarious; she was popular and made friends easily. In the main, she expected others to be as friendly and pleasant to her as she was to them. One thing that was reckoned by some to be a fault in her was a tendency not to take things seriously enough. She was certainly very quick to spot the ridiculous if it was manifest. Occasionally she was sharp-tongued, but she had enough self-awareness to recognize if she had offended and was quick to apologize with what she was told was a beguiling sweetness.

This long sea journey to India she thought a fabulous adventure. It wasn't costing her a penny. She was competent both with a needle and sewing machine and there was plenty of inexpensive material available in Romford, so she had made most of her own clothes in preparation for the journey. This meant that the money the firm had given her had stretched amazingly; she even had cash to spare. She felt not only independent, but liberated. There would be nobody to answer to for six wonderful weeks. Her husband was in West Africa, her boss awaiting her arrival in Calcutta, and her parents in Scotland. She had never felt so carefree.

10

Ship Life

*D*ays on board passed pleasantly. Coffee and tea were served mid-morning and mid-afternoon. There were deck games when the weather permitted and general friendly conversation. Initially the weather was unpleasant – grey skies and greyer tormented seas – but after a week or so it became altogether warmer. Although there was still a slight swell and the ship rolled a little, after the roughness of the passage through Biscay it was perfectly tolerable, and very pleasant to be in the fresh salty air. Moving about the ship was no longer a real problem and more and more of the passengers were venturing onto the deck.

Miss Phelps did crosswords to which she admitted being almost addicted. Mary was happy to sit in the sun under a parasol and chat. Mrs Harrison knitted endlessly and, whenever she could, roped someone in to hold a skein for her. Mary's bold and abrupt departure from Dunoon intrigued her. "I think you were brave," she said one afternoon, "but a little foolhardy. How old were you?"

"It was 1935, so I suppose I was about twenty-two. But I felt I'd been there long enough, so began to look for something else. My parents of course were horrified; even Glasgow was a step too far in their opinion." Mary knew she was speaking with an overtone of bitterness. She knew she didn't want to talk about Michael.

Ted Boddle, a young army captain sitting beside Mrs Harrison, a skein of wool stretched between his hands, grinned at her. "Well, Maisie McCutchion, tempted by the bright city lights, I suppose?" She had once let her maiden name drop into conversation; the mood lightened.

"I don't remember giving you permission to use my family pet name. I hate it anyway. If you are going to be this familiar, can you call me Mary?" She spoke cheerfully and without embarrassment.

She saw Mrs Harrison raise her eyebrows as she looked at both of them over her glasses. Mary returned her glance with an innocent smile. Mrs Harrison was not an inquisitive woman but told Mary later that day that she had decided to make discreet enquiries about Captain Boddle, in case her young friend was being "led astray".

"I do *know* he's married, Mrs Harrison," Mary said. She had decided not to be cross or irritated by what she might have felt was impertinence when she was gently told of his status. "So am I. I am sure you have my best interests at heart. Don't worry; this is companionship, friendship; it's not even a shipboard romance. He's good fun and," leaning forward, she added with a grin, "more importantly, he plays darts!"

She was aware that there was a certain amount of speculation among some of the other passengers. All these people were gathered together in what was in reality a small closed world. Gossip about all sorts of things floated around, adding a frisson to an uneventful time. She knew herself to be innocent, so ignored the knowing smiles and occasional silence when she entered the lounge or bar with him, or deliberately chose to sit in an adjacent chair. Her outgoing nature allowed her to be friendly with several of the officers aboard, and if she had a partiality for Ted Boddle, it was no more than that. She was polite and reassuring to Mrs Harrison but the QA who was unwise enough to comment got short shrift and was frozen out. She got another page to herself in Mary's shipboard diary.

The weather continued to get warmer and the lounge was abandoned as the outside decks filled with passengers reading, chatting, or sunbathing. People mixed well and there was a relaxed holiday atmosphere. Sometimes from the troop deck below there were sounds of the naval ratings being drilled and the chatter would diminish to allow the orders to be given without a hubbub of noise from above.

The crew changed into white tropical kit, as did the servicemen – at least those who wore uniform. Formal dress was de rigueur for the evening but during the day there was a motley collection of apparel. Casual flannel trousers began to make an appearance, together with aertex shirts. Some of the younger, more daring men wore shorts, but as these were banned from the lounge, bar, and above all from the dining room, their wear was limited.

Mary was both touched and grateful, on returning to her cabin one evening to change for dinner, to discover that Billy had collected her modest collection of summer dresses, skirts and blouses, and ironed them all. He had also found coat hangers, and hung them all up, summarily shifting the QA's uniform to her side of the rail.

The crew made great efforts to keep boredom at bay, so there were organized team games during the day, where everybody cheated openly and unashamedly. In the evening, there might be a singsong around the out-of-tune baby grand piano. Sometimes there were quizzes, a magic lantern show, or tombola; some enthusiastic players started a bridge club. Occasionally there were talks. Some were interesting, others less so. Mary felt that the subject matter was less important than the delivery. The most prosaic subject could be enjoyable if the speaker was articulate, dynamic, and fun. She particularly enjoyed one about growing a prize-winning marrow so large that it had to be taken to the exhibition hall in a wheelbarrow. This would not normally have been a gripping topic but in this instance, bulked out with amusing anecdotes, it passed a very pleasant hour. Most things she felt could be reasonably enjoyed in a comfortable armchair with a couple of whisky and sodas.

The best evenings were when a film was shown. The projector was unreliable and broke down regularly so the result was often erratic. The resulting barracking was taken in good part by the projectionist, usually the purser, who invariably managed after a moment or two to get the film on track again. Cowboy films were enjoyed and anything with Charlie Chaplin, Clark Gable, Carole Lombard, Madeleine Carroll, or Robert Donat was wildly popular. *The Thirty-Nine Steps* was shown two nights running by popular demand. The blackout curtains in the lounge made it very hot but everyone was prepared to put up with it if it meant they could enjoy the escapism of the cinema.

Every day people crowded round the daily bulletin posted outside the purser's office. The details were general rather than specific: air and sea temperature, the weather outlook, changes in the sea condition, the entertainment, the time and date for the next lifeboat drill. The first lifeboat drill took place the day after sailing. There was a belief, among those clustered round the notice board, that security was the reason for the lack of detailed information. Someone even mentioned the possibility of spies aboard a British ship out in the Atlantic. This distressed the gentle Miss Phelps, who was horrified that any one of the charming and, she believed, patriotic passengers or crew could be guilty of such duplicity. Mary was amused at her naïvety but saw her distress and was at pains to comfort and reassure her. Some of the naval personnel had worked out the position of the ship but were discreet in the distribution of this knowledge.

The weather indicated that they were a good way down the west coast of Africa. She also noticed that the other ships that had set off with them had disappeared. Ted Boddle confirmed that they were no longer being escorted by the naval frigates that had accompanied them when they left Liverpool on 11 March. Mary had become used to their reassuring distant grey outline, one to port and one to starboard. The ocean seemed very empty without them.

On 22 March a dance was held on the troop deck, and all the female passengers, married or single, were politely requested to attend in order that the young naval ratings could have the opportunity of dancing. This was the usual procedure on ships where there were predominantly men aboard. It was always important to keep the men occupied and entertained, as boredom made for short tempers.

Mary put on her one long evening dress and did her hair and make-up carefully. She fastened her amethyst thistle brooch to her shoulder and looked critically at herself in the mirror. She felt quietly pleased with her appearance. "Goodness," said her unfriendly cabin companion, who was lying on her bunk reading. "Don't you look smart! It's only for the men, you know."

"Well," said Mary, with more politeness than she felt, "they are young and far from home. We have been asked to go, and it seems a very small thing to me, to give them a few hours of our time to alleviate their boredom. You, I take it, are not going?"

"Goodness, no! We are excused, you know, as we are officers. I hope you enjoy yourself." She picked up her book again and groped with her hand for the whisky on her locker. Mary looked at her and thought how deeply unpleasant she was. There was nothing else to say. She was angered by the insolence and the snobbishness, both of which she thought completely unwarranted, and furthermore not worthy of any comment.

In the lounge, she joined Mrs Harrison and Miss Phelps. The former wore a surprisingly elegant cocktail dress, and the latter an eau-de-Nil crêpe de Chine blouse and long skirt.

"I shan't dance," Miss Phelps confided. "I don't know how to really, but I thought I'd go. I mean we ought to, don't you think?"

"Yes, I do," replied Mary firmly, "and I expect to have a very nice time indeed." Ted and a couple of his friends escorted them down.

The event was well organized. The deck was dressed with bunting, which lent some colour and gayness to the drab blackout. The men all behaved with great civility. There was no alcohol served, but instead a delicious fruit drink. There was no unruly behaviour. A wind-up gramophone provided the music. The young men were a little shy at first but with the encouragement of the non-commissioned officers in charge soon began, if rather bashfully, to ask the women to dance. Mary saw that all the other army nurses had come. Unsurprisingly almost all the young men were beautiful dancers, their apprenticeship having undoubtedly been served in the dance halls, the Palais de Danse, found all over Britain. Because there were so many men and so few women, the women were never without a partner – even Miss Phelps was encouraged onto the floor. The dance ended at 11 p.m. and Mary and Ted, together with some others, went up to the bar on the passenger deck. They played rummy for about an hour and had a few drinks before turning in.

Back in her cabin, Mary undressed quietly and hung her long dress up. She unclasped the thistle brooch with its pretty amethyst stone that Michael Brogan had given to her that sunny Sunday afternoon as they sat beside the reservoir above the town, and put it into her beautiful dressing case. The memory was mixed with pain. Why, she wondered, was she thinking so much about Dunoon? She hadn't seen Michael for five years, yet this was the second time in as many days that she found her thoughts turning not to London, but to Scotland.

Interlude

"Your voyage sounds like great fun!"

My mother didn't answer for a moment and seemed lost in a world of reminiscence. She lit a cigarette and inhaled deeply.

"Yes, it was fun. It was another world. It was like being in a vacuum; it was all so light-hearted. Do you know? I don't think for a moment anyone ever thought about us being in one of the most dangerous places in the world. We were in a sort of time capsule, a little bubble of nonchalance. Except of course people didn't use expressions like that then. It seems ridiculous now, but I felt safe."

"Well, there were no bombs falling, no Blitz, and no air-raid warnings. What about food: were you rationed?"

"That's funny; I can't really remember. I suppose the ship with the Goan crew ate a lot of Indian dishes. I do seem to remember a lot of lentils and vegetables but as I like lentils it wouldn't have bothered me. Food isn't really that important to me. I can't say I remember a scarcity of meat, butter, or sugar. I think we ate well. I seem to recall there was lots of ice-cream."

My mother always gave the impression that talking about food was somehow vulgar. As children, my brother and I were forbidden to make any comments at the table about what we were eating. Even to say something was nice was frowned upon. Her attitude to food was reflected in her cooking, which was dreadful: Bisto gravy with everything. Yet she was a good baker and produced wonderful sponges and shortbread. At Christmas she made fabulous black buns, a cross between Christmas pudding and fruit cake, the whole thing encased in pastry. She began assembling the ingredients about September and made them in November. One year she made ten and distributed them to family and acquaintances. Both her parish priest and her doctor got one. The latter said he made his last until March he enjoyed it so much. The cakes managed to stay perfectly fresh, thanks to the bottles of cognac that she poured in after they were baked.

11

Ship Life Continues

*M*ary sat on the edge of the bunk and looked ruefully at the bottom of her long dress. The dance had done some damage. Not only were there about eight inches of undone hem but there was also a jagged tear where she had caught her heel during a reverse turn. Having looked hopefully for some blue thread among her very small supply of sewing things and found nothing that really matched, she decided to go in search of Mrs Harrison, whom she thought was the most likely person to be able to help. Then, as she passed the purser's office, it occurred to her that given the amount of blue uniform about, repairs must be undertaken by naval personnel. The purser laughed and produced a spool of blue cotton.

"As if by magic!" said Mary, gratefully holding out her hand.

"Just a minute, Mrs Stewart; there's a forfeit. Could you sew on three buttons for me and – dare I ask? – there's a hole in one of my white socks. I could probably manage the buttons but the darning defeats me."

As she walked away with his shirt and the socks over her arm, and mending materials in a small envelope that he had produced, he called out, "By the way, how are the darts teams coming on?"

"I've got ten positives and about another four or five possibles, so I think it'll be fine. When's the match again?"

"The twenty-seventh, so you've got time."

She tossed over her shoulder, "I'll let you have these things back before dinner. It'll be our little secret; don't tell anybody else – I don't want to be inundated with mending."

Back in her cabin, she was a little disconcerted to find her disagreeable companion apparently asleep on her bunk. She had secretly hoped that she might perch there to do the mending but, rather than clamber aloft to her own bed, she hauled her cabin trunk out into the only available space, found scissors, needles, and a thimble, sat down and began work. She sewed the buttons on swiftly, put the shirt aside, and then turned to her dress. She pinned up the hem and threaded her needle with some difficulty, as the light was poor. She became aware gradually that she was being watched. Suddenly the other woman spoke.

"How beautifully you sew: such tiny, tiny stitches. Do you make all your own clothes?"

Surprised at this unexpected verbal interaction, Mary smiled. "A lot of them: dresses, skirts and blouses – you know… not suits or coats."

To her knowledge, these were the first civil or even friendly words the nurse had addressed to her, and she was at a loss as to how she might best respond. The last thing she wanted was a snub.

"I can't sew for toffee," the other sighed. "Neither my mother nor my nanny ever taught me. Anyway, there was always someone else to do it." Then abruptly she asked, nodding to the small photograph of Colin that Mary kept propped on top of her dressing case, "Is that your husband? Where is he?"

"In West Africa, with the Royal West African Frontier Force. He's training troops."

"Gosh," the nurse sat up abruptly. "That's a cushy war!"

Although Mary could hardly deny the truth of it, she was rendered speechless by the rudeness and could only look at her. Then, to her astonishment, the nurse began to cry. After a moment or two, Mary got up and found a handkerchief, which she handed to her. The girl took the handkerchief with a muttered "thank you", then after a moment she carried on haltingly, "I'm so sorry. What you must think of me, I can't imagine. You see, both my brothers were killed at Dunkirk, and I find it really hard when I know of others who aren't..." And she began to cry again.

"Colin's time may well come," said Mary grimly. She didn't think it appropriate, even in the interest of solidarity, to wish her husband in a more dangerous situation than he was currently in, but she spoke gently. "I am sorry for your loss. To lose such beloved people must be dreadful."

It would have been good, she thought later, if this unburdening of herself had led to a more pleasant relationship between them but unfortunately, having revealed the possible cause of her antagonism, the nurse reverted to her previous aloof manner.

"Poor girl," said Mrs Harrison with easy sympathy, when she heard the tale. "Grief sometimes puts iron in the soul. I shall pray for her; we all ought to do so. None of us knows what lies ahead." Mary wasn't sure whether she could bring herself to pray for such a disagreeable companion but decided that the least she could do was make some gesture towards civility. So next morning, when Billy brought in the tea, she called out cheerfully, "Good morning," and had the satisfaction of hearing a grudging response.

Mary knew the purser had disregarded her request not to pass the word about her sewing prowess when one of the Roman Catholic priests and then an RAF officer came to her after breakfast with mending requests. At lunchtime these were followed by others, including, to her surprise, from two of the QA nurses. Mary had assumed erroneously that all women learned to sew. She realized she would need to augment her supply of threads and wool if she were to take on the unofficial role of seamstress. Secretly she was pleased; she hated to be idle and she enjoyed sewing.

12

Attack

*T*he two captains, Mary thought later, must have watched each other across the pewter-grey Atlantic. Not so very different in a way: pursued and pursuer, hunted and hunter; like dogs circling each other, stiff-legged and bristling. Aboard both vessels, tense, patriotic men, a little fearful, were clammy-handed and dry-mouthed, sweating in anticipation, the air thick with its own particular odour of excitement or apprehension.

The call to action stations would have actually calmed the crew; given them a sense of purpose. *Thor*'s captain watched the smoke and *Britannia*'s zig-zag evasive course, while *Britannia*'s captain eyed uneasily and with growing scepticism the Yugoslav flag flying from *Thor*'s stern.

It was 7:15 a.m. Just over six miles separated the ships. *Britannia*'s larger size and more powerful engines gave her the advantage of speed. Uncertain as to the nationality of the vessel doggedly tailing her, she decided on making a run for it and began to make smoke and steam away. *Thor*, fearful that she would lose her quarry, abandoned all pretence and set off in unmistakable pursuit. Over a short distance the pursuing vessel was confident of catching up. On the bridge, *Britannia*'s captain watched grimly as the Yugoslav flag was struck and the crooked cross of the swastika was hoisted on what was indubitably an enemy vessel.

Below deck, *Britannia*'s passengers and the crew not on duty, oblivious to the drama unfolding above their heads, slept peacefully in their bunks. They were not to rest long. At 10,000 yards, with the *Britannia* in range, *Thor* opened fire.

Mary was jerked awake by the noise of the shell overhead. She knew instantly what it was. It was all too horribly familiar. She had no idea if the first one had struck its target, but the second and third certainly did. The ship shuddered and groaned like an injured animal. There was the screaming of tearing metal, the acrid smell of cordite and then the deafening sound of *Britannia*'s single gun returning fire. She could hear large objects falling onto the deck above and had no idea whether these were shells, bombs, or damaged superstructure. It generated a bowel-loosening terror. Whatever they were, she certainly didn't want to be caught beneath them.

The ship's sirens began to sound. She felt that the noise, which reverberated through her like electricity, was worse than the shelling, which became continuous. Her own fear generated a rush of adrenaline. Her hands tingled and her breath rasped in her throat. Tossing back her bedclothes and dropping down from her bunk, she was on her feet almost before she knew it. Her cabin companion, who was always an early riser, stood paralysed by the washbasin, toothbrush in hand. Mary had the mad impression that the girl was foaming at the mouth and wondered for an instant if she was having a fit until she realized it was toothpaste.

She let out a gasp of almost hysterical laughter then, reaching into the cupboard, pulled out underwear, a pair of slacks and a jumper. She struggled into her clothes. The immediate fear gone, she felt no panic, only urgency, yet it was difficult to control the trembling of her hands. She found them slimy with sweat, and pulling on her shoes was difficult. Grabbing her coat, handbag, and life jacket from the back of the door, and stuffing a sunhat into her pocket, she stepped out into the passage. She looked at her watch: it was 7:50 a.m. The whole business of getting dressed and out into the passage had taken about three minutes.

Looking back into the cabin, she saw her companion still standing, brush in hand, her mouth un-rinsed. "Come on," she shouted, "we're under attack. Get a move on. You must get dressed as quickly as you can! Forget your bloody teeth." She had the satisfaction of seeing this advice galvanize her companion into action.

Outside in the corridor there was a crowd struggling towards the stairs, some still in their nightwear and some, she saw to her dismay, without their life jackets. "Is it a practice?" a man asked. Someone gave a bark of laughter. Nobody asked that question again. There was a considerable amount of bad-tempered and frightened jostling to get up the stairs. In that restricted space the air was heavy with the smell of sweat and morning breath. Outside the purser's office, the ship's doctor, his blood-stained white coat pulled on over his pyjamas, straightened up from a body over which he had pulled a towel. He caught Mary's eye, gave a caricature of a smile and moved on to join two nurses who were attending to other badly injured crewmen, one of whom was groaning horribly. Through the open door leading outside, she saw several bodies; the deck was awash with blood. With horror she wondered how many more there were of them below. She felt her gorge rise and her mouth flood with saliva.

The purser began to direct people through the double doors leading into the main lounge. He was very pale but perfectly composed and reassuring; he smiled but kept saying firmly, "Please keep moving; please go through." There seemed a curious reluctance for the first people to do so, but once they had breached what they appeared to feel was a hidden barrier, they began to shuffle forward. Others followed, like sheep, Mary thought. A man standing next to her had a handkerchief held to a wound on his temple. She saw, with disgust, that blood from it was dripping onto her shoulder. She was ashamed, thinking she should feel pity or compassion rather than revulsion. She remembered, unbidden, the line from Macbeth "Who would have thought the old man had so much blood in him?" He reassured her that it was only a graze, although she saw clearly the flap of skin torn from his scalp.

She wished they would turn off the sirens and almost at that moment, as if her thoughts had some power, they fell silent. Momentarily the shelling seemed to have stopped.

The purser directed, "Will everybody please lie down on the floor." With some reluctance, people obeyed. The carpet smelled unpleasant and was rough and rather sticky. She shifted her face from it so that her cheek lay on her hand. She wished that she had been to the lavatory before going upstairs, and wondered if she could make a dash for it and use the one on the landing by the purser's office. The discomfort in her bladder was insistent but she told herself it was just nerves and decided to try and ignore it.

She found the close proximity of so many bodies disagreeable. A large army officer lay next to her, his hip and thigh pressed unpleasantly, if impersonally, against her. He kept mumbling, "Steady, steady." She wasn't sure if this was to reassure her or whether it was a mantra to comfort him. She thought the latter; he seemed oblivious to her, lost in his own unsettled world. On her other side was a young airman, green with fear, the sweat beading on his forehead, his hands quivering. She put her other arm across his shoulder and felt the trembling of his body. "It'll be OK," she assured him, with considerably more confidence than she felt. Then attempting cheerfulness, "Guess what? It's my birthday today."

He gave a ghastly travesty of a smile. "Did you have anything planned?"

"Well," she replied ironically, "certainly not this." She had no idea how long they lay on the carpet – perhaps half an hour. Some people became restless, and one man even got up to peer through the window. "I can't see anything," he complained. The purser shouted angrily to him to lie down.

The shelling started again and the ship was hit time after time. There was a terrible persistent shuddering below them. Mary felt it up through the carpet into her own body as if she herself were being struck. Sometimes, when a shell found some particularly vulnerable target, *Britannia* almost seemed to leap from the water. There were sharp cries of fear and she heard someone sobbing, a dry, hacking, gasping noise. After a while there was a pause in the firing followed by a prolonged ominous silence. The ship, she realized, was no longer moving.

The tannoy crackled into life and they heard the captain's voice. He sounded very composed.

"May I have your attention. We have been attacked by a German vessel and have sustained considerable damage. We are no longer able to manoeuvre, nor to defend ourselves, as our gun has been put out of action. Consequently, I am giving orders to abandon ship. Please make your way calmly to your lifeboat stations. God bless you all."

Outside on deck there was no panic but considerable confusion. Several of the lifeboats on the port side had been damaged and were swinging from one rope so that they banged hollowly against the side of the ship as she rolled in the swell. Others had holes and were not seaworthy. There was a great deal of indecisive milling around as people were arriving at their lifeboat station only to be directed to another.

Mary saw Mrs Harrison and Miss Phelps among those crowding about Lifeboat Number One – one of those damaged and clearly unusable. She waved frantically to them, "Over here, over here!" Miss Phelps had her life jacket over her nightdress, and slippers on her feet. She looked completely bewildered. The two women, by means of pushing determinedly through a solid wedge of bodies, eventually reached Mary, and the three of them struggled their way to Mary's allocated boat. The second officer, Lieutenant Frank Parker, was at the station.

Mary watched her two companions clamber with difficulty over the side and down into the lifeboat; Miss Phelps, giggling nervously, was hampered by her long nightdress. Avoiding Lieutenant Parker's hand, Mary hissed, "I've got to use a loo." Her need to urinate now that she was upright was urgent. He gestured with his chin to the far side of the deck.

"Nobody will notice you, Mrs Stewart. Use the fire bucket, but be quick – we are almost full here; I'll save you a place." Such was the urgency that she obeyed immediately, indifferent to the several passengers who saw her pull her slacks and knickers down. She thought for one uncertain moment that, in her nervous haste, her bladder would freeze and she wouldn't be able to go at all, but it didn't and her relief was instant. She struggled back to her station and found Ted Boddle beside her. To her astonishment, he offered quite seriously to go below to her cabin, to fetch her beautiful dressing case, Dr Maxwell's leaving present. She stared wordlessly at him.

Lieutenant Parker gripped her arm and handed her up and over the side. She felt a complete sense of unreality. A small stepladder descended into the lifeboat. She went down carefully and found a seat immediately below it. The last two people to follow her down were Lieutenant Parker and Ted Boddle.

The boat swung out and began to drop. At one point a davit jammed and the boat lurched. There were cries of fear. Parker hit it sharply with a hammer and it freed up. The boat continued its descent and suddenly they were afloat. Mary saw to her amazement that the surface of the sea was covered with debris: deckchairs and other furniture, unidentifiable pieces of spar, ropes, sheets of paper, books and files, and dance records still in their brown covers. Where had it all come from? she wondered.

A small table bounced disconsolately by, with its legs in the air. Beyond it floated a couple of rugs and a considerable amount of linen. Unexpectedly and incongruously, a lavatory seat was flung into the air by a wave and, as it fell, it struck the side of the boat. Mary saw the colourful bunting that had decorated the deck at the dance floating carelessly among the mess. She felt suddenly overwhelmed with sadness and fear and began to quiver. Ted, feeling her shudder, leaned round her and put a piece of chocolate in her mouth. Instantly she was violently sick and managed just in time to turn her head to throw up over the rail.

Three or four other lifeboats bobbed up and down beside them. Lieutenant Parker called out to let fall the oars which Mary understood meant for them to be placed in the rowlocks ready for rowing. This caused initial confusion as people were actually sitting on them, and the subsequent struggle to free them made the boat rock alarmingly. Water slopped over the gunwales. People cried out in fear, grabbing each other and shouting angry warning complaints. By the time the oars were set the other lifeboats were some distance off. With two men rowing strongly, they pulled away from the ship.

The sun was coming up and the day felt warm. Suddenly and unexpectedly, a small motorboat appeared from out of nowhere and circled the stricken ship.

"It's the enemy, looking to make sure all the lifeboats are off," someone ventured.

"Or to pick up survivors more likely; not everyone got into a boat." Parker's voice was calm but dispassionate.

All heads turned anxiously to follow it. Mary saw a man swimming strongly towards a raft. The little motorboat caught up with him easily and hauled him aboard. "Lucky him," said another voice, with a grim laugh.

Someone standing in another lifeboat about 200 yards away began to semaphore. "What do they want?" queried Ted.

"They are very low in the water," said Lieutenant Parker, "and want us to take some of the women off. I can't help them. My responsibility is only to this boat and if they panic we'll all end up in the sea!" Mary noted the rigid clasp of his hand on the tiller and thought she could feel the tension this decision was causing him. He saw her troubled face and smiled reassuringly at her.

The little motorboat disappeared and the shelling from the enemy vessel began again. "Where is it?" asked Mary. "Where is it? I can't see it." She kept turning her head and twisting round. She felt she would have been less frightened if she could see the raider. There was something terrifying about this hidden assault.

"It's about three miles or so away," replied Parker, "but we are well within its range. It's been following us for some time, since about 3:00 a.m. actually."

The shelling began again. All eyes were fixed on *Britannia*. Mary began to feel light-headed. *It is like some terrible dream*, she thought. *In a moment it will all be over, and I shall be back in my bunk waiting for Billy to bring me my morning tea.*

She lost count of how many times the stricken ship was hit. As they watched, hideously mesmerized, almost disbelievingly, she began to sink slowly on an even keel, lower and lower into the water. Surely, this pleasant vessel where only yesterday they had been so light-hearted did not deserve this ignominious fate. Suddenly her bows went down and she upended. For a long moment, they saw her screws, silhouetted black against the morning sky, like a reproachful hand raised in warning or farewell. She began slipping down vertically and a plume of flame, smoke, and steam shot several hundred feet into the air. Then, unbelievably, with an appalling gurgling roar, she was gone. The surface foamed, seethed, and bubbled at the point of her disappearance. Nobody spoke. A great pall of silence and horror hung over them all. The rowers continued to pull away and after a very short time the other little boats vanished and they found themselves quite alone.

13

The Boat, Day 1

*M*ary tried to take stock of who was in the lifeboat with her. Apart from Mrs Harrison and Miss Phelps, there were few she had met. She recognized the Roman Catholic priests and was happy with Ted Boddle and Lieutenant Parker's reassuring presence. Further down the boat she thought she identified the quartermaster and some of the Goan stewards. She hoped to see Billy the tea steward but could not spot him. There were some naval ratings that she thought she vaguely recognized. Perhaps she had danced with them, she mused. The rest were strangers, haphazardly thrown together by misfortune.

The bouncing motion of the little boat was unpleasant, particularly if a wave hit it broadside, when it would judder and then roll. The motion was so unpleasant that Mary, a good sailor, was surprised to feel seasick. Looking around her, she saw she was not alone. Ted seemed fine but poor Miss Phelps was in some distress, as were several of the Goan seamen. One of the Roman Catholic priests was vomiting regularly and copiously over the side, either from fear or from nausea, or perhaps both. *Thank God he isn't in the middle of the boat*, Mary thought, *at least his neighbours are spared being sprayed with puke*.

The lifeboat, which had seemed so comfortably large when they had practised their lifeboat drill, now seemed very small indeed and was seriously overcrowded. There wasn't an inch to spare. Mary wondered who had estimated the number of extra passengers over and above the forty that the lifeboat would comfortably accommodate. Clearly, Lieutenant Parker thought that the fifty-six now jammed together shoulder to shoulder was the maximum. He had even been prepared to sacrifice the nurses in the other boat – a very tough but necessary decision.

Looking around her Mary thought how blank all the faces looked. Dazed and confused, they all seemed in the grip of a sort of communal shock. She didn't hear anyone speaking. Everybody sat in a remote bewildered silence. The unbelievable disappearance of what, a short time ago, was a solid, reassuring, comfortable home, had left them all stunned. Everything was gone: clothes, books, personal possessions, family mementos, everything!

After a short while, adrift and alone, Lieutenant Parker stood up and called out, "I am sure you are all wondering what's going to happen." There was an eager movement, heads turned towards him. He smiled at the expectant faces and cleared his throat. His voice, a little reedy at first, gathered strength.

"The first thing to tell you is that the captain managed to send out a signal that we were under attack. Although the enemy tried to block it, we heard Sierra Leone responding, so our situation and position have been recognized. We are in the shipping lanes and I have every expectation that we will be picked up."

There were some half-hearted cheers at this. "However," he continued, "the contingency plan is this. We will sail due north for a week in the hope of reaching the Cape Verde Islands." He ignored the gasps of horror. A week! It seemed horrendous, unbelievable; hadn't he said they were in the shipping lanes? Mary wondered wryly how many people had actually thought they would be picked up before lunch. "If we don't reach them," Parker continued, "we will sail due west in the hope of reaching the African coast. What we have to do now is ascertain if we have a sail to fit our stubby little mast, and I am afraid I must ask some of you to move carefully, as I believe it is amidships, underneath where we found the oars."

It was a difficult job to raise the mast and took patience and considerable manoeuvring. One of the Goan crew got his fingers jammed and dislocated two knuckles. Miss Phelps, in a pause between vomiting, re-set them and then tore the lace off the bottom of her nightie to strap them up. She was terribly, wrenchingly sick once more after this effort, then smiled shakily across at Mary, who was watching her with sympathetic anxiety. Wiping her mouth with the back of her hand, she said firmly, as if to stiffen herself, "Right, that's enough of that."

The search for a sail produced a poor, frail piece of canvas, but Parker said cheerfully, "That's better than nothing." So the sail was rigged, which meant that the rowing was only supplementary. Provisions of water, boxes of dry biscuits, and unmarked tins were discovered in the forward locker. The tins were found, astonishingly, to contain condensed milk.

"The water and biscuits," Parker said, "will be issued twice a day. It won't be much but it will be adequate. In the meantime, please take your life jackets off and hang them on the hooks over the side. This will give you all a little more space."

His calmness and authority were deeply reassuring. Mary decided he was only about twenty-five and could only wonder where this quiet confidence came from. She felt her spirits rise under his direction and, glancing around, saw how earnestly and trustingly all the pale faces were turned towards him. They hung on his words, like children taking a parent's hand, confident that they would be led to safety.

"All able-bodied men," he smiled at the three women, "the ladies are excused, will take two-hour watches." Then he concluded, "Please don't put your hands in the water."

"Why ever not?" Mary asked, startled.

Ted Boddle explained, "Because when you are thirsty, the cool water on your fingers produces a terrible temptation to suck them – a bad thing to do. Salty water is not to be recommended as a thirst quencher."

After this little speech and the erection of the mast, people seemed to settle down. There was a general wriggling as they sought for a more comfortable position or, rather, a less uncomfortable one. The benches were hard and those amidships had nothing to support them. Mary, at the stern and the side, at least had the hard taffrail to lean on, to ease her back.

After the terrifying scramble into the boats, the horror of *Britannia*'s monstrous end, and the dreaded uncertainty of what was to follow, an uneasy calm settled over them. This was soon followed, inevitably, by an awareness of the deadly monotony of their situation. Despite a clear and, Mary thought, British willingness to make the best of it, there was nothing to see, nothing to do, and ultimately nothing to say. The general quietness was unnerving but strangely soporific. All around her people sat with closed eyes. Exhausted with emotion, she too found herself drifting into a sort of reverie, and felt her head dropping onto her chest, and her eyelids drooping. She wondered, momentarily, if dying would be this easy. She could have stayed like that for hours and was actually relieved to be shaken out of it by Lieutenant Parker speaking to her. She was astonished to find it was nearly noon. The sun was high and it was very hot. Reaching into her pocket, she pulled out her sunhat, which gave her some relief.

"Mary," Parker said, "I am going to put you in charge of the provisions. Everyone will get half a ship's biscuit twice a day. I want you to spread them with the condensed milk. Of course," he added, with a laugh tinged with slight bitterness, "they haven't provided anything helpful like a tin opener. But I wasn't a Boy Scout for nothing and I can open the tins with a knife, which fortunately I have!" He produced a serviceable penknife from his pocket.

"When shall I start *buttering,* if that's the word?"

"Straight away; it will take you some time."

He was correct. It took nearly two hours to cut the biscuits in half and spread them with milk. It was a very disagreeable job. She had only the lid of the biscuit tin as a table; it was not easy to cut the biscuits in exact halves, and her fingers were soon sticky with the milk. Parker's penknife was the only implement available and not very efficient, the blade being too narrow.

Whoever did the stocking of this vessel, she thought crossly, *was seriously lacking in imagination and practical good sense*. The effort involved in her task seemed to drain her and when she was finished, she felt unable to eat her own share.

"Please try," Ted cajoled her. "We are going to need all our strength."

"Alright. I will when I've had a drink."

From the bows of the boat where the water supply was stowed, a young seaman made his way very slowly up the narrow passages between the seats. Round his neck he had a chain with a very small scoop, little bigger than an eggcup, on either end. He was carrying the demijohn of water, which had a small tap in it. As each person was served two scoops, he had to stop to refill before moving on. Everyone watched with painful eagerness. The wait for those in the stern was interminable. It took nearly an hour to reach them. The water was tepid and had an unpleasant taste and it didn't quench Mary's thirst but she drank it eagerly and then managed to eat her biscuit.

The afternoon dragged on. There was no relief from the sun. The sea was calm and shivered with a silvery glare that was hard on the eyes. Those on watch found it both exhausting and painful. Few people, in their haste to leave the dying ship, had brought sunglasses with them.

Sometimes shoals of little flying fish burst from the water, their fins iridescent. People who had watched them with cries of pleasure a day or so back glanced at them with indifference. The heat was intense. Mary saw that the tops of her feet in her canvas shoes were beginning to burn and she asked the man nearest her if he could pull down the turn-ups of her trousers.

She was so tightly wedged she was unable to reach them herself.

Towards 5 p.m. she began her food preparation again and there was another ration of water.

Mrs Harrison put up her hand to attract Lieutenant Parker's attention and asked quietly if she might say a prayer. He nodded. She produced a little book from her pocket and began to read:

"I will never leave thee nor forsake thee. And, behold, I am with thee, and will keep thee in all places whither thou goest, and will bring thee again into this land; for I will not leave thee, until I have done that which I have spoken to you of [Genesis 28:15].

"So that we may boldly say, The Lord is my helper, and I will not fear what man shall do unto me [Hebrews 13:6]."

Although her voice was not loud, it carried softly across the bowed heads. She read the lovely words with intense and impressive conviction, then folded her hands, closed her eyes, and lowered her head. Beside her Miss Phelps smiled at Mrs Harrison and then kissed her cheek. It was a moment of great tenderness.

"Thank you, Mrs Harrison," said Parker quietly. Further down the boat someone began the Lord's Prayer and there was a general murmur of accompaniment. With the cooling of the evening, a blanket of tranquillity seemed to settle over the boat; an easing of anxiety, and a softening of the stress. A kerosene lamp was fitted to the mast. It glowed dimly. The light it shed was barely discernible from one end of the boat to the other, but it afforded a strange comfort. A light shining in the darkness, Mary thought with a weak smile.

The sun dropped lower in the sky, its yellow glare turning pink as it began to sink towards the horizon until it finally disappeared in a fiery flare of orange. Almost immediately, it was dark.

Mary thought she had never seen such a beautiful starlit night. The heavens seemed ablaze with light. She looked up at the constellations above her. Then hesitatingly she looked at Parker and then looked heavenward again to make sure she was not mistaken. The Plough, immutable in its placement, showed the path to the North Star. She twisted her head trying to line it up with the mast and saw immediately the discrepancy.

She felt a pulse jumping in her throat. "Lieutenant Parker, Frank," she said quietly. "We are not sailing due north at all. It seems to me we are considerably west of north. On this course I don't think we are going to reach anything."

He didn't speak for a moment, then he took her hand and said carefully, "Listen to me. You are young and fit. You will be able to survive a great deal, and although this is a dreadful ordeal, I am sure we will be rescued. After a few days you will forget all your terror and distress. This will seem nothing more than an amazing adventure. You are right: we are not sailing due north but are being pulled to the west by the trade winds. We *will* be picked up. *Britannia*'s signal was received and acknowledged. People are looking for us. In the meantime, don't throw your life away in despair."

She listened, clinging to his hand, and when he had finished speaking, she turned her face into his shoulder and wept.

14

The Boat, Day 2

*T*he night was bitterly cold, but astonishingly Mary managed some sleep. It was fitful but Ted pulled her against his side and put his arm round her. Exhausted, she drifted off. She woke each time the watch changed and saw that others, like her, were managing to get some sort of rest. Miss Phelps had actually slid off her bench and was curled up at Mrs Harrison's feet, a remarkable achievement for such a tall woman. Her head was on that good lady's lap. Lieutenant Parker didn't seem to sleep at all. Whenever Mary opened her eyes and peered blearily around, he was alert at the tiller.

The sunrise had them all awake and the little lamp at the masthead was doused. By consensus morning prayers were said. Then the dreary round of preparing the biscuits and condensed milk began again. *I will never again use condensed milk*, Mary assured herself, revolted by her sticky hands. She remembered that as an adolescent in America, her Aunt Bessie used it to make a creamy dessert called lime tart, which at the time Mary had thought delicious. She promised herself that she would never eat it again. Even the memory was enough to induce nausea. Thirst was becoming an issue and the long wait for water was harder and more difficult to bear. People were patient, but the tiny ration did little more than wet the mouth. It certainly didn't assuage the thirst.

The watches changed with monotonous regularity. At least this activity produced some diversity, as it involved people moving around, stumbling over complaining bodies and reformulating the sitting placements. *At least we are alive*, Mary thought, *if we complain about a stubbed toe*.

Halfway through the morning, the investigating of other lockers threw up what was originally thought to be another sail. This turned out to be a tarpaulin which, when rigged, gave some relief from the pitiless sun. It didn't cover everybody, so was re-rigged every two hours so that all had some shade at some time in the day.

Peering over the side, Mary thought she saw elongated torpedo-shaped creatures just below the surface. She shuddered. "Are they sharks?" she asked Parker fearfully.

Before he could reply, a pod of dolphins shot to the surface, racing along beside the boat, their beautiful, sleek, streamlined bodies glistening with water. They stayed with them for some twenty minutes, leaping and plunging. It was a joyous, playful exhibition. One was so close she could have touched it. As it turned away for the last time, Mary saw its large placid eye. It was very close and gleaming. She thought it looked directly at her with benign reassurance. The comfort that the presence of those beautiful creatures brought her was something that helped her through that interminable day.

In the afternoon the wind dropped and the movement of the boat became sluggish. Lieutenant Parker, in his capacity as captain of the boat, announced with some reluctance that all able-bodied men must take turns in rowing. "Initially," he said, "for half an hour at a time."

Mary was surprised that this directive caused some emotion. There was a small rustle of resentment, of grumbling.

"Where are we rowing to?" The speaker, a fair, wan-looking man, was truculent. He stood up looking round for support and Mary saw there were a few heads nodding in sympathetic agreement. Sitting almost motionless for so long had induced a sort of indolence in everybody. Nobody really wanted to move.

Parker was patient but Mary could see by the expression on his face, with his lips firmly compressed and knuckles white on the tiller, that he wasn't prepared to be challenged.

"We shall hold the same course in the expectation of being picked up. We *could* sit here with a slack sail for days, using up our limited supply of food and water, but I don't think that's a good option. So we will row, and we will stop rowing when the wind picks up."

Then he added wryly, addressing his interlocutor, "As you are on your feet already, perhaps you would like to be one of the first. I will choose your companion." There was some laughter at this and the fair-haired man took the rebuff in good part, preparing to accept the situation. His fellow rower was the Roman Catholic priest who had been so sick on the first day. He had been an Oxford blue and initially the movement of the two was very uneven but, under instruction, which was accepted willingly, they began to make a little headway.

"We could do with a better cox," said the priest, "but keep the tiller steady and we'll manage."

"I'm the only cox you've got," said the helmsman. "Just keep rowing."

Turn and turn about, the boat was rowed through the day and into the evening. Thankfully the wind picked up just before sunset, almost immediately after Mrs Harrison had completed her evening prayer.

"Perhaps we should have prayed sooner," suggested Ted.

"I'm praying all the time," said Mrs Harrison with a smile, and Ted nodded his approval.

The ration of biscuits spread with milk and the small scoops of water were issued again. Thirst had become acute and the longing for water dominated everybody's thoughts. The little lamp was hung on the mast. The sun sank just as before and night fell.

Mary's face felt very sore and was, she suspected, sunburnt. Her lips she knew were swollen and blistered. Miss Phelps, with her pale colouring, was suffering too. Someone had given her a hat, so her face was to some degree sheltered, but her arms were crimson. At night, on the other hand, in a thin nightie, Mary thought she must have been terribly cold. Why ever, she wondered, hadn't she put some clothes on when the alarm went?

Once again, she looked up at the starry night with some wonderment. Again, it was dazzling. That second night there was a shower of shooting stars, a rapturous pyrotechnic display. As if, she thought, the heavens were offering some compensation: a reward for suffering the dreadfulness of the day. She remembered how she had, as a child, lain on the grass with her father while he pointed out the constellations to her. She thought how much he would have appreciated what she was seeing. She was sorry he wasn't with her. This childhood memory, which rose to the surface, pierced her with anguish. Determinedly she tried to avoid looking at the Plough. She was sure they were veering further to the west.

That night, she felt she did not sleep at all. Thirst, the discomfort of her sunburn, and the bone-aching cold kept her from rest. Looking around at all the faces pallid in the moonlight, she saw that others were in the same state. People were beginning to slump against each other, heads nodding on unresponsive shoulders. Not for the first time she thought of death. The night seemed endless. She tried to remember Parker's words – "Don't throw your life away" – but they seemed somehow insubstantial. She couldn't cry and wondered if it was because she was so dehydrated. She hadn't urinated either since using the fire bucket, a lifetime away. She had no desire to do so but thought her kidneys might be suffering.

Then, just when the siren thoughts of despair began to seize her, it was dawn. The sun came up and the tatty little sail billowed out with wind. Another day gave hope of salvation. Perhaps today, or if not maybe tomorrow, their rescue would come.

"Breakfast time," she said ironically to Ted, and opened the biscuit tin.

15

The Boat, Day 3

*S*preading the condensed milk, she had no time to look around until finally the job was done. Mary became aware of a decided change in the atmosphere among the "castaways". People's expressions were not just lethargic but indifferent. Yesterday there had been more normal reactions. People had tried to accommodate each other, shifting if they could, to share the restricted space. They had expressed some relief when under the relative shade of the tarpaulin. They had smiled at the dolphins alongside the boat. There had even been the odd desultory conversation. On that third day the mood was darker and even sullen. People avoided looking at each other, seemingly isolated and lost in their own little world. Food, but above all drink, was becoming an all-consuming craving. With parched mouths, it was hard to chew and swallow the biscuits, even with the added sugary milk. Mary saw that several people refused them. She herself was tempted, but Ted spoke brusquely again about needing to keep her strength up. A ridiculous idea, she thought: she had no strength at all to keep up.

A whale passed close to them and as it surfaced, it blew out a huge gust of steam and water. It sank below the waves and then resurfaced closer. Perhaps curiosity drew it in. Even this, which would, under other circumstances, have generated interest, comment or perhaps alarm from the passengers, did not even merit a passing glance. One of the stewards trailed his hand in the water, causing the only event that broke the monotony. He cried out in pain when it was bitten or stung by some unidentified creature. The first aid box was rudimentary: a few bandages, sticking plasters, a bottle of gentian violet, a triangular sling, and some cotton wool. It contained nothing that would have been any use for a serious injury.

"It clearly wasn't a shark," Ted remarked, "else it would have taken his hand off."

The quartermaster suggested it was a jellyfish sting and anointed the man's hand with gentian violet. He was grimacing and moaning in pain. The rest of the boat stared at him with indifference. His discomfort only seemed to cause annoyance, and one or two made grumbling complaints. "Oh, do shut up! It's only a jellyfish!"

"Serve him right," said Parker, grimly and unsympathetically. "He should have obeyed instructions. I said not to put your hands in the water."

The steward was holding his hand above his head; clearly this afforded him some relief. Looking down the boat, all Mary could see was the purple limb waving as if he were trying to attract her attention. She felt an almost irresistible desire to wave back.

The previous day someone had suggested that a swim might help to alleviate the discomfort of the intense heat. The sea had been calm and sparkling, and if one forgot, just for a moment, that the boat was virtually adrift in a vast deep ocean, with the seabed several hundred feet below, the idea of splashing about in the water as one did at the seaside was more than appealing. Mary, a good swimmer, had been appalled at the idea. "Are they mad?" she had asked Ted. "This is the Atlantic, not Weston-super-Mare."

"Anyone fancy a swim *today*?" Ted nodded towards the steward's purple hand and then pointed over the boat's side. Mary glanced down and saw with disgust a pulsating mass of umbrella-shaped medusa surrounding them. Some were more than a foot in diameter. There were hundreds of the creatures, the sea thick with their revolting, gelatinous presence.

Toward evening Mary sensed her concentration going. Two or three times she found herself gazing dreamily into the distance, her hand suspended, condensed milk dripping from the blade. It was becoming a struggle to prepare the food, and Ted and the Catholic priests helped her. The priest broke the biscuits and Ted spread the milk. He tore off the back of a small official-looking notebook that he had in his pocket and used the cardboard cover as a knife. The red dye came off on the milk but nobody complained.

"I'm destroying military equipment. It's probably a court martial offence."

"I think there are extenuating circumstances," volunteered Parker, reassuringly. "I'll stand as a character witness."

Mary looked dreamily at the torn notebook and thought of her diary. She imagined the ship sinking down until it rested on the seabed. She saw her book, its pages loosening, gradually detaching themselves, then floating, oscillating down through the flooded cabin to settle gently on the floor, a watery grave. The pages would disintegrate, she knew, but the words on the pages might slip free from the paper and out through the smashed porthole, drifting up through the water to the surface. She hoped perhaps that the words would come back to her. Staring calmly into the distance she thought she saw the curling and looping symbols of her shorthand, like so many little black moths. They were airborne, and danced towards her in the glimmering sun, insubstantial but tantalizingly clear. She even put out her hand to catch them, only to find them evaporate as she reached for them.

Ted, seeing her glazed eyes and waving hands, pulled her against his shoulder. "Easy, old girl," he said. "Easy now."

"Do you know what today is?" she asked Ted, coming to with a jerk. She felt a bubble of hysterical laughter rising up.

He shook his head.

"It's the day of the darts match."

They clutched each other, both giggling helplessly while those nearest them stared in sullen bewilderment.

Toward nightfall, the weather began to worsen, and just before the little lamp was fixed to the mast, Lieutenant Parker asked that lifejackets be put on. Not everybody had one. Some had slipped from their hooks and been lost. One of the naval ratings stood up and yelled that he didn't care. "If I am going to be swept overboard, I'd prefer it was quick, rather than me floating around for hours among jellyfish and sharks." There were mumblings of agreement.

"Any more of that sort of talk," the quartermaster shouted in response, "and I'll throw you in myself. Now sit down and shut up!" A little buzz from the others could have been laughter, approval, or despair.

The wind picked up and the sea became increasingly rough. It was a hideous and fearsome night. No watches were changed; standing up was impossible. The moon appeared intermittently from behind the scudding clouds but it was no comfort, for it only revealed the rolling waves with their menacing foamy crests. The boat was buffeted about and creaked and groaned as if in the grip of some monstrous sea beast. Everybody was seized by terror. People clung on to each other for reassurance, comfort, and security. Occasionally waves broke over them, and when eventually daybreak came and the wind dropped, they were all soaked and shuddering with cold. The only reassurance during those long relentless hours was the little hurricane lamp, which (quoting from *The Merchant of Venice*) "Like a good deed in a naughty world" had continued to glimmer bravely.

16

Rescue, Day 4

*T*he boat sat lower that morning of the fourth day because of the water it had shipped in the night. Eventually a small pail was unearthed from another locker and, together with an empty biscuit tin, the boat was bailed out. The job was disgusting, for not only were the bilges full of seawater but also of vomit, a result of the turbulence in the night. Worse than that, there was also a quantity of human waste.

"Please!" Mary pleaded. "Can I wash my hands in the sea? They are so revoltingly filthy." Lieutenant Parker nodded his approval. "I don't think I can do the biscuits," she added. She was exhausted to her very core, her arms and back aching, her hands trembling.

He smiled very kindly at her and touched her shoulder gently. "Captain Boddle and the padre will help you," he said.

Then turning away from her he looked with some anxiety at the two missionaries sitting slumped against each other. Shakily Mrs Harrison returned his smile. He said bracingly, "Come along, Mrs Harrison; morning prayers as usual please." With some effort, she pulled herself upright.

People sat with bowed heads, sunk in a kind of stupor, and when she finished, there was no accompanying murmur but an apathetic silence. Nobody volunteered the Lord's Prayer either.

Miss Phelps had tentatively begun, "Our Father…" when there was a sudden heart-wrenching cry from the watch.

"Ship on the starboard beam!" Slowly, unbelievingly, every head turned. Very faintly against the horizon there was the dim grey outline of a ship. A ripple of tense excitement ran through the boat, a quiver of hope and expectation. Nobody could really believe what they were seeing, and yet…

"Nobody stands up!" shouted Lieutenant Parker. "Nobody stands up." He had his binoculars fixed to his eyes. He raised his hand and signalled to the quartermaster, who scrabbled frantically in a locker to find the flares. His hands shook so much with excitement and nerves that he could barely light one. Eventually he succeeded and a moment or so later it shot into the sky and blossomed. It hung in the air like an enormous Christmas decoration, orange smoke streaming from it. Then it dropped down and sank into the water.

Parker kept his glasses trained on the distant ship. "He's holding his course," he said. His voice was steady. He signalled for another flare to be fired and then a third. Some people began to shout out, their cries a mixture of fury and despair.

They must see us, Mary thought in anguish. *They must, they must.*

Parker took off his jacket and asked the priest to pass the hurricane lamp and an oar. He tied his jacket to the oar, poured the kerosene over his jacket, and set it alight. It blazed fiercely. He held the oar above his head, ignoring the pieces of flaming material dropping around him. Below it, in the little boat, fifty-six people sat motionless, their eyes fixed on what they hoped against hope would be deliverance. Then the silhouette of the distant ship changed and foreshortened as she turned her bows to the south and began steaming towards them.

"Yes," said Parker, grinning. "Yes, they've seen us." There was a collective sigh of rapture and then a vocal outburst of amazed relief. People burst into laughter, and hugged and kissed each other in delight. Everyone began to shout in excitement. The company, which such a short time ago had been sunk in despair, was alert and expectant.

Parker announced, "If anyone wants a drink of water you may have as much as you wish."

Astonishingly, nobody did.

The idea crossed Mary's mind as she watched her rescuer approach that it might be a German ship. Well, if it is was, they would be prisoners, but at least dry and fed.

It was astonishing how quickly their deliverance arrived. In no time, it was alongside them. SS *Raranga*, they later learned, was a refrigerated ship on her way to pick up produce for Britain from South America. As a British merchant ship, she was also a target, but with a small crew, even if she had been identified, the Germans might well have decided there were richer pickings elsewhere. She was lucky; Mary learned later that merchant ship losses were horrendous. That wonderful day, the survivors of Mary's boat saw smiling, welcoming faces peering at them from high above. Then several ropes snaked down and the lifeboat was secured against the ship. It towered above them. Mary thought it was like looking straight up the side of an immensely tall building.

"The women will go first," directed Lieutenant Parker. He signalled aloft and a bosun's chair, a kind of sling, was lowered. Mrs Harrison was hoisted first. Miss Phelps, almost naked in her nightdress, was lent a jacket for decency by one of the others and then she too was hauled up.

Watching the dangling legs and the expanse of thigh exposed by the process, Mary thought, *No German is going to subject* me *to this indignity*! She declined the chair and when the rope ladder was lowered and secured, was the first to go up.

"Are you sure you can manage?" Ted asked anxiously.

"I don't think we need to worry about Mrs Stewart, Captain Boddle; she's tougher than she looks," Lieutenant Parker assured him. He steadied the ladder and, taking her hand as if leading her onto the dance floor, handed her up onto it. "Up you go, chef," he said, grinning at her. She hung her handbag round her neck and grasped the rope.

It was a long climb, and halfway up she began to wonder if she had made a wise decision. After only a very few steps, the muscles of her thighs and calves burned and her hands slipped on the rope. The ladder, despite being held steady below, swung out from the ship occasionally, causing her to gasp with fear. It was very hard work but she clung on grimly and mounted slowly. At the top, hands reached for her, grasped her arms and shoulders, and pulled her up into the boat, where she sprawled exhausted, face down on the deck. Gently she was helped to her feet and a cup of tea was put into her hands. She had never tasted anything so delicious. Her cup was immediately replenished.

Mrs Harrison and Miss Phelps were already in deckchairs, the latter made completely decent now with a blanket around her. "For the entire world," Mary told them, "you look as if you are on a boat holiday." She felt hysterical with relief. When she grinned, she felt the burned skin crack on her cheeks and didn't know whether it was tears or moisture from the blisters that was running down her face. She crouched down beside them and peered into their faces and they smiled back in return but didn't speak. They both looked very weak and exhausted.

There had been a serious deterioration in their condition in the previous twenty-four hours. Miss Phelps's arms and legs were badly sunburned. Her expression was strained and she was sunken-eyed. Mrs Harrison looked in slightly better shape, although Mary noticed the swollen legs and the trembling hands. Both had bruised cheeks from being thrown roughly against each other during the storm. The two women stared wordlessly at her as if their dreadful experience had left them dumb.

Mary was filled with a mixture of compassion and triumph. "We've survived," she said. "We're safe. As you said, *All will be well, and all will be well and all manner of things will be well.*" She had the very distinct impression that the words were meaningless for them at that moment. She took their cups gently from their hands and went to get more for them to drink.

Sweet tea was served to all the filthy, exhausted, sunburned men as they arrived. She watched them stagger aboard and was astonished at the variety of immediate behaviour. They milled around, shaking hands and yelling with delight. Some hugged each other, several wept. Some shouted with laughter and burst into conversation. Many were silent. One of the priests fell to his knees, kissed the deck, and then seemed lost in private prayer. Finally, the last few struggled aboard. Looking over the rail Mary saw that only the quartermaster and Lieutenant Parker remained in the boat.

Parker leaned over the side and prised the name SS *Britannia* from the bow with his knife. It was the same knife, Mary realized, she had used to "butter" the biscuits. Tucking the nameplate under his arm, he followed the quartermaster, holding the compass and binnacle, up the ladder and they both eventually stepped onto the deck. They were calm and composed and went round everybody to congratulate them and to thank them for behaving so correctly. They were very gentle with Miss Phelps and Mrs Harrison, speaking quietly and reassuringly to them. The quartermaster offered three cheers for Lieutenant Parker and everybody hurrahed. Mary thought it was such a British thing to do, but was truly touched.

Standing at the rail with her tea in her hand, and distancing herself from the crowd, Mary watched the cockleshell that had saved them, bobbing away from the ship. She followed it with her eyes as it drifted into the distance. This little boat, anonymous once its name had been removed; this frail insubstantial vessel that had brought them to safety, was now abandoned, its job done. Eventually, as she watched, it floated further and further away, until it became a tiny dot in that huge ocean, and then suddenly it was lost to view. The lump in her throat was so huge she could barely swallow her tea.

She was startled out of her emotional farewell by a hand on her arm. She turned to find a naval officer standing beside her. He was a small man, very smart, with a delightful smile. "Mrs Stewart, I am Captain Starr, in charge of this ship. I am putting my quarters at your disposal and those of the two other ladies. There are only two bunks in my cabin but I have given instructions for a further camp bed to be installed. There is a shower room and I have made sure that there is everything you could need. In due course I will have your clothes laundered for you."

Mary looked at him, blinking her tears away, and began a halting reply. She felt a little dizzy and swayed. He took her gently by the elbow.

"You need rest," he said. His voice was compassionate. "You've been through a terrible ordeal. Your two companions have retired. I suggest you do the same." He guided her across the deck.

"What about the others?" she asked anxiously.

"They are fine. They are all taken care of. Now go to rest."

In the cabin, the curtains were drawn and the room was dim. It was peaceful and somehow comforting. There were towels and cotton bathrobes on a chair beside Captain Starr's desk. Mrs Harrison was stretched out on one of the bunks, Miss Phelps kneeling beside her. Neither of them looked up when she entered. Mary thought they were praying and felt a very strong inclination to join them.

Through one of the doors leading from the cabin she found the shower. Without hesitation, she stripped off her clothes, which were stiff and damp with salt. She caught sight of herself in a mirror and stared in horror. Her face was burned and peeling, her lips cracked and swollen. In the shower she stood, letting the tepid water gush over her, washing the salt from her face and head. She felt it streaming down her back and over her breasts, down her torso to her feet, washing away the sweat and grime of the last few days. Her face stung and smarted but she made no effort to avoid the stream. After a while, she rubbed her head and found it free from salt water. On the shelf, she found Drene shampoo which she had used herself at home; it was surprising to find it in a man's bathroom. She thought that maybe his wife got it for him. The lovely foaming sensation of the hair wash was an exquisite pleasure.

When she stepped back into the cabin wrapped in a towel, her hair still damp, she found both her companions fast asleep on the bunks. On the camp bed there was a pillow and a sleeping bag. On the captain's desk was a large carafe of water, three glasses, and a jar of Vaseline with a note beside it: "Recommend you drink plenty of water. The heads [the toilets] are beside the shower room. Please use the Vaseline on your sunburn. Put your clothes outside the cabin and they will be laundered. Sleep well. Robert Starr."

Mary finished drying herself, smeared Vaseline onto her face, hands, and the top of her feet, drank a big glass of water and wriggled naked down into the sleeping bag. Looking at her watch, she saw it was 2:30 p.m. Faintly, she heard voices outside on the deck, occasional laughter, and then she slipped down into blissful oblivion.

Interlude

I was considerably shaken by the detail of her account of the sinking of SS *Britannia*. I had known about it, even as a little girl, though she spoke of it very rarely. Here was my tiny mother, at this time in her life only about four foot ten (at her tallest five foot and a half inch – and very proud of that half inch), so strong, so courageous. I was caught up in her story and anxious to know what long-term effects this dreadful event might have had on her.

"I've been listening to Tape 5," I said. "About the sinking and that terrible, terrible time in the lifeboat. Did you have nightmares? Did it come back, terrifyingly, in dreams? Did it haunt you? It was, after all, a horrendous experience."

She responded immediately and with vehemence. "I never dreamed about it; not once. I thought about it a great deal afterwards though, although I rarely shared my feelings. You cannot convey an experience like that to others. You cannot make them feel what you felt, what you lived through: the terror, the despair, the thirst, the discomfort. 'How dreadful,' they say, 'it must have been ghastly.' 'Yes, it was,' you answer but you know they can't really understand. So I rarely talked about it afterwards – neither about the sinking, nor the time in the boat – not until I made the tapes. What did trouble me was the thought of the injured who sank with the ship. That caused me anguish. All those doomed men, knowing their fate, going down to their watery grave. Nevertheless, in the last few years I've changed. I felt a compulsion to get it down and as I can't type any more, I had to record it all. I believed that I had a story that needed telling. I was surprised myself how immediate it felt."

I sensed a pride in her about the events but I could also tell by the hesitation in her voice that she really didn't want to dwell on it. So we passed on to something else and she talked cheerfully about the SS *Raranga*, the boat that saved them.

17

SS Raranga

𝒯he SS *Raranga* was bound for Montevideo, something of an inconvenience for the passengers of the SS *Britannia,* who had embarked in Liverpool for passage to Bombay and onwards. Mary was philosophical about it, and, now she was safe, even allowed herself to be amused about this unlooked-for turn of events. Mrs Harrison was in a frenzy of anxiety. Her husband had been due to meet her on arrival in India. It was impossible to send any kind of signal from the SS *Raranga* without betraying their position, so the ship kept radio silence.

"He won't know what's happened to me!"

Mary pointed out that as they would arrive in Uruguay at approximately the same time as they were due in Bombay, she would be able to send a reassuring signal once they had docked.

"Yes, but he'll be in a terrible way, wondering how I am managing in Montevideo. We haven't any money. What will we do? What about our passports?" Like many, she had obeyed the purser's recommendation to destroy all identification papers. It was only a recommendation and Mary had decided that this was a ruling better kept in the breach than in the observance, and her passport was safely tucked into the inner pocket of her bag. It had been difficult enough to acquire it initially, and she was determined to hang on to it if she could. Despite the outside of her bag being soaked with seawater, her documents had remained relatively dry inside.

"I am sure that there will be British officials to help us. Uruguay is neutral; we won't be abandoned on the street. Remember what the captain said."

Captain Starr had convened all *Britannia*'s passengers the day after their rescue. He told them that the ship's loss would be known and as soon as they were in neutral waters, he could send messages. He assured them that the British government had representatives in Uruguay who would take care of them. Mary wasn't sure how this would be handled, but she was still too weary to ask for further details and was content to trust the captain's knowledge.

She was impressed at the tolerance the crew of the SS *Raranga* showed their fifty-six uninvited guests. Their own laundry was put on hold until the passengers' clothes were cleaned. Mary considered that most of the burden of their presence fell on the cook, who had twice the number of mouths to feed.

"How will he manage it?" asked Miss Phelps.

"With great ingenuity," replied Mary, laughing.

The main problem was the lack of space. During the day the decks were crowded with men, as there was nowhere else to sit. There was a great deal of squabbling over the few deckchairs available. Mary considered that the behaviour of the former castaways was worse than when they had been packed together like sardines in the lifeboat. At night they crowded either into the SS *Raranga*'s cabins, sleeping on blankets on the floor between the bunks, or on the benches in the little mess. The crew's own quarters were small. Unlike a passenger liner, the living area below deck was very restricted. Yet the crew remained affable: smiling and helpful.

Mary and her two companions realized how very good Captain Starr had been to give up his comfortable and private quarters for them. While their clothes were being laundered the two missionaries wore the cotton bathrobes. The captain bashfully presented Mary with a pair of his own shorts and a cotton shirt.

"I think these might fit you, Mrs Stewart. They may be a little large and a little long but I think they'll do." She was touched at his thoughtfulness. Someone found Miss Phelps a pair of cotton trousers and a steward's jacket. The trousers were too short and the jacket drowned her, but she was finally decent. She had to stay in her slippers until someone found her a pair of canvas deck shoes. They were too small but she cut the toes out. She threw her nightie away, saying she never wanted to see it again.

One afternoon Captain Starr came to join the little group around Mary.

"You know," he said conversationally, "we saw you three times before we came for you."

"You mean we could have been picked up sooner?" Miss Phelps sounded appalled, her normally quiet voice shrill with disbelief.

"I'm afraid so. We saw you the previous evening, before the big storm, then twice the next day, but it could have been a trap. The third flare and whatever it was you were burning convinced us."

Mary remembered with horror the dreadfulness of the third night. She thought of the storm, of the sheer terror she had experienced, of the certainty that she was going to die. She looked at him with bitter reproach.

"I'm sorry," he said, "but we had to be sure. We came as quickly as we could once we were certain."

"Do you know about any of the other boats?" asked Ted. "Have they been picked up?"

"I don't know, but it's very possible. There were several ships in the area."

Lieutenant Parker had told Starr that when SS *Britannia*'s captain had radioed that the ship was under attack, not only had the message been picked up by Sierra Leone but also by a British warship, which had been coming at full speed to help.

This was the reason, Parker felt, that the German boat had left the scene so quickly and, with one exception, the swimming man, had not picked up survivors.

The SS *Raranga* was still eleven to twelve days out of Montevideo. In an effort to keep boredom at bay, various schemes were dreamed up. Quizzes were devised and were played with aggressive competitiveness. Charades were very popular because so many could participate. Mrs Harrison was very good at guessing but when it was her turn, the books she chose were so obscure that the participants became impatient. Everybody expected her to choose *The Pilgrim's Progress* or *The Imitation of Christ*, but instead she chose *The Private Memoirs and Confessions of a Justified Sinner* by James Hogg: a book so esoteric that nobody had heard of it. When Captain Starr found several packs of greasy, dog-eared playing cards these were seized with enthusiasm.

Mary and Ted made up crosswords, drawing a grid and taking turns to fill in a letter. They laughed and squabbled and appealed constantly to others for verification of completely made-up words.

"Of course *foxable*'s a word! Isn't *foxable* a real word, Miss Phelps? It's like gullible. Someone is so naïve they are completely *foxable*."

"If you are allowed *foxable* I'm having *trint*."

"You can't just have *trint*; you've got to define it!"

"OK; *trint*: meaning, very irritated by someone. Like, I was feeling pretty *trint* about your refusal to accept *trint*."

Mary threw a cushion at him and went off to write her diary. Captain Starr had provided her with a small notebook and a pencil and she wrote frantically for two or three days, anxious to record in the greatest detail the events of the past week. Everything seemed important. Nothing was too insignificant. She was reluctant to lose any of those momentous moments. The events themselves pressed in on her with an emotional charge that she was desperate to capture. Sometimes and unexpectedly she found tears on her cheeks as if the recall had touched something very profound in her. The thought that she had escaped death when others had undoubtedly perished caused her real anguish. She wondered if the nurses were safe and thought for a moment with compassion about her haughty cabin mate. Had she survived?

Months later Mary learned of the rescue of other lifeboats. One was an extraordinary tale. A British vessel picked up the boat crowded with the nurses. When they boarded the ship one of the nurses discovered that the medical officer on board was her own father! Another boat was picked up by a Spanish vessel and taken to the Canaries, and yet another made a desperate twenty-six-day voyage, ending up on the east coast of South America. More than half of the passengers on the boat died on that terrible journey. But that knowledge was in the future.

Sitting scribbling away in her notebook, Mary reflected with anguish on other things. Was the swimming man pulled into the German patrol boat being well looked after? What had happened to the seriously injured people, like the ones the doctor had been tending? Did they take the injured into the lifeboats or did they go down with SS *Britannia*? She rather feared the latter. She remembered the inadequate first aid kit. How could one look after seriously injured people with gentian violet and sticking plasters? Maybe Lieutenant Parker would know. But she lacked the courage to ask him.

Interlude

All my mother's tapes were interesting, but the two that covered the sinking and the time at sea were the most dramatic. For some days after listening to them I found myself looking at this tiny birdlike woman and trying to imagine her thoughts and feelings about that time; the things she didn't reveal. I felt there must have been a multitude. Her determination to record it all in her diary – the three frantic days of writing – indicated, I thought, how reluctant she was to forget anything.

Yet it was strange. She had put it out of her mind for half a century and now there was this tremendous outpouring. Perhaps she felt her mortality and realized that all those memories would be lost if she didn't recall them in a concrete fashion.

"I think something of me went down with the *Britannia*," she told me one evening. "Is that fanciful? I don't think I was ever completely the same person afterwards. I looked at life differently."

It didn't seem unreasonable to me. I was to think more about this when I heard later tapes.

18

Montevideo

*Th*ere was both excitement and relief when they arrived in Montevideo, sixteen days after the sinking of SS *Britannia*. Everybody crowded along the rail to look at the wreck of the German battleship *Graf Spee*. Her captain had scuttled her at the mouth of the harbour, much to the fury of the Uruguayan government. Her superstructure was clearly visible above the water.

Mary saw Captain Starr looking down at it with sadness in his face.

"A beautiful ship." His voice was quiet. "Lovely lines; she burned for days." He was silent for a moment. "I was a prisoner on her, you know. She'd sunk a lot of ships but no prisoners were killed or ill-treated. All the Allied prisoners, and there were quite a few of us, were released, and all her crew sent ashore before her captain, a man called Langsdorff, opened the sea cocks and then set fire to her. He was a real gentleman: he lent us books when we were his *guests* and made sure we had cigarettes. He spoke perfect English."

"Why did he do it?" enquired Ted. "I mean, scuttle her?"

"Well, we fooled him. He thought they were barricaded in and that there were several British ships just waiting for him to leave harbour. It was all a rumour. There were just three cruisers, and the *Graf Spee* could have out-run them. It's called disinformation."

"Why didn't they just stay put?"

"It's the international rules of war, Mrs Stewart. Ships at war only have twenty-four hours to stay in a neutral port. If they are seaworthy, they must leave. Presumably he felt he had no alternative. Obviously he believed Herr Hitler would not understand, so he shot himself in a hotel bedroom. I was very sad when I heard. He was a man I liked."

"But an *enemy* ship, Captain Starr!" After her own recent experience, Mary was not inclined to feel any sadness or sympathy.

Starr smiled. "Look at it this way: ships are not enemies; it's people. A ship is just a ship." He looked out again at the masts and funnel of the wreck. "Anybody that loves the sea and ships can only feel sadness at that sight. Yes, of course it's good that she is not out creating havoc and mayhem in the Atlantic, but still it's a sorry end for a beautiful vessel."

It was a bedraggled group that disembarked from the SS *Raranga*. Most of the men, after nearly a fortnight without easy access to a razor, were unshaven. Nobody had any possessions other than the crumpled clothes on their backs. Captain Starr told Mary and Miss Phelps that he was happy to make a gift of the things he had lent them. In Miss Phelps's case, this was something of a necessity, as she had nothing else to wear.

On the dockside they were jostled by reporters, but as advised by Lieutenant Parker and Captain Starr, they refused to speak to any of them. Staff from The Mission to the Seafarers gathered up the Goan stewards. Others, including the Catholic priest and the handful of naval ratings, disappeared to a variety of lodgings or temporary accommodation. An official from the British Embassy collected up the remaining British contingent and took them to the Hotel Alhambra. This was a large and imposing building in the old town, dating, Mary guessed, from the beginning of the century. The rooms were enormous and sumptuous and she was pleased to have one to herself. The bed was deliciously comfortable after the spartan sleeping arrangements on the SS *Raranga*. Mary didn't think she would miss the camp bed at all. She did remember with a smile, though, the almost sensual pleasure she had experienced, when, after four days in a lifeboat, she had snuggled down in her sleeping bag between the rigid poles and canvas base of her makeshift bed.

The group gathered in the hotel lounge beneath vast chandeliers, surrounded by heavily gilded rococo ornamentation. The Embassy official told them that as it was Holy Week, the week leading up to Easter, most shops in this conservative Catholic country were closed, but that one department store had opened just for them so that they could buy essentials. The Embassy would meet the bill. At least, Mary thought, she could brush her teeth again. A toothbrush was something that Captain Starr had not been able to provide and she had been forced to scrub at her teeth with the corner of a towel, which was better than nothing but far from satisfactory.

It was about six o'clock before they reached the store and already dark. After the blackout at home the lights dazzled them. It was another world. Everybody found it difficult to decide what counted as a necessity. A toothbrush, a change of underwear, nightclothes, a hairbrush were obvious, but what of soap? Mary couldn't remember if there had been soap or shampoo in the bathroom back at the hotel. Nobody else could remember either. She took some just in case. Miss Phelps agonized over face cream: was that necessary?

"I should jolly well think so," said Mary, finding jars of her favourite, Ponds Vanishing Cream. "With your fair skin, it's an absolute essential." She dropped two jars into Miss Phelps's basket.

The following morning they made their way to Thomas Cook, relieved to find it open in the morning. Mary sent a cable to Dr

Maxwell at May & Baker. She knew that she would be sent a money order and hoped it wouldn't be too long. She needed clothes, having become tired of wearing baggy shorts and slacks. She left her address with the office and they promised to contact her as soon as there was any reply.

That second evening she and Ted went out to explore the district. The old town was very beautiful with fine classical and colonial buildings and pleasant open squares. The whole place was alive with people strolling around, couples arm in arm, and small children playing. The atmosphere was charming, the evening balmy, and it was with quiet contentment that they sat down on a bench to watch the world go by. They commented with pleasure on the sights and sounds of the plaza. After some time, she began to notice that people were staring at her, not very pleasantly, and obviously talking about her. She was at a loss to know why. Some older women positively scowled at her.

"Whatever is it?" she said, puzzled. Disturbed, they got up and decided to return to the hotel, avoiding the more populous areas. They turned into a side street and passed a severe, military-looking building with a short flight of steps leading to an open door. Above it was the Montevideo coat of arms. It was a police station. Two officers came down the steps and moved towards them. They looked serious. One of the police officers held up his white-gloved hand to stop them. He said something that neither she nor Ted understood and then repeated it more loudly and aggressively.

"I'm sorry, old boy," said Ted, with all the insouciance of the Englishman abroad, face to face with Johnny Foreigner, "I don't speak Spanish." This failure to be intimidated resulted in them both being hustled into the building. There were several police officers inside who broke out into an increasingly threatening verbal outburst. They kept gesturing at Mary, who began to feel seriously alarmed.

"It's your trousers," said Ted suddenly. "They don't like your trousers!"

She groped desperately for something to say about why she was wearing a garment so clearly disapproved of, and suddenly shouted, "*Náufragos*" (Spanish for castaway). She thought later she must have heard the word from one of the waiters at the hotel. There was a sudden complete silence and then an outburst of "*Náufragos, Náufragos. Lo siento mucho.*"

There were smiles and apologies all around. Chairs were brought out and then a bottle was produced and several glasses. With a great display of affability and much slapping of Ted's back, drinks were pressed on them. It was very fiery liquor and made Mary gasp, but, reluctant to provoke more recriminations, she gulped it down. Her glass was promptly refilled. She laughed and thought, *Why not?* Ted drank his with evident pleasure. The police officer showed him the bottle: it was white rum. As they were drinking and toasting each other – by this time the arresting officer had his arm around Mary's shoulder – an older and apparently more senior officer entered the room. He spoke good English. "I must explain. Here in Montevideo women don't wear trousers in the street, especially not during Holy Week. Trousers are for the beach or holidays or even sailing, otherwise they're considered disrespectful, unwomanly! You were in the plaza, yes? There were complaints. Of course now we understand."

The two of them were escorted back to the Hotel Alhambra with every courtesy.

What larks, thought Mary. *I hope May & Baker sends me some money soon. I've obviously got to get more clothes.*

The next day all three British women received an invitation, or rather a summons, to tea with the British ambassador's wife, Lady Effie Millington-Drake. As they were escorted up a wide flight of stairs inside the residence, the official said, "Lady Millington-Drake is a little indisposed today and hopes that you will forgive her receiving you in her bedroom."

Inside a large and elegant room they found their hostess. She was a very small woman with a bright, animated face and dark curly hair. She welcomed them warmly, apologizing for her "indisposition" but was not specific about it. Mary thought she looked fine, indeed in better form than Mrs Harrison who, these days, seemed curiously shrunken and diminished. The calm, smiling, confident woman that Mary had come to admire on the SS *Britannia* had turned into an anxious creature, jumpy and indecisive. She herself was well aware of this, and had hoped that rest and the considerate care she had received on the *Raranga* would have restored her, but she remained tremulous and apprehensive. She and Miss Phelps both confessed to having dreadful nightmares and sleeping badly, although the latter was recovering steadily. None of them really felt up to this sophisticated interaction. In the light of their recent experience, it seemed inappropriate. They sat uneasily on chairs stationed around the bed.

Tea was served, with tiny sandwiches and exquisite cakes. Mrs Harrison said afterwards that she had felt so guilty biting into all that gorgeous food when she remembered how tough life was at home. The luxuriousness of the room contrasted shockingly with their own shabbiness. Miss Phelps's pink and bony shins were barely covered by her trousers, and Mary's own slacks were in need of a pressing.

Conversation was initially a little stilted. Lady Millington-Drake said, "Please tell me about your amazing and terrible adventures. I am so happy for you all that you survived. I cannot imagine how dreadful it must have been. Have you been in touch with your families?" She seemed genuinely interested in them and in their plans. Gradually the whole odd situation became easier. They all laughed when Miss Phelps said that, actually, none of them had any plans as they had not yet made contact home. Their hostess seemed genuinely shocked and said, "I'll tell my husband to hurry things along!"

Lady Millington-Drake, whose personality was three times larger than her bird-like body, overwhelmed them with her restless dynamic energy. Mary thought she must be exhausting to live with. She discovered later that in fact her warm-hearted generosity made her a very popular ambassadorial wife. She was also known for her extravagance. All her clothes came from the French fashion house of Worth. Many of the clothes made for her were to her own designs, and she sent for them via the diplomatic bag. They were presumably delivered the same way.

Just before the end of the visit, having studied her three guests intently, Lady Millington-Drake threw the bedclothes back, leapt from her bed, and flung open the wardrobe doors. Her clothes were exquisite. "I can't do anything for you two, sadly," she said, eyeing up the two missionaries. "I've nothing that will fit. But you, Mrs Stewart, I *can* help."

She invited Mary to help herself to anything she wanted! It was a moment of exquisite embarrassment and when Mary, protesting, declined, Lady Millington-Drake selected two dresses at random. One was a lilac linen shift and the other a pleated tussore afternoon frock, both quite beautiful. Mary stammered her thanks, which were dismissed with an enchanting smile and an airy wave of the hand. A label on the neck of the dresses identified their provenance: "WORTH". A maid was summoned to wrap the clothes. While they waited for her return, two scarves and a handbag were pressed on Mrs Harrison and Miss Phelps. She brushed their embarrassed thanks aside. "I can't let you go with nothing," she announced. The women then left what they felt had been an audience chamber. They were exhausted.

The English expatriate community began to descend on the hotel in some numbers. They were very kind and ready to help. Invitations to tea and dinner were pressed on them, but Mary was left with the strong impression that they wanted to lionize all the survivors. The latter were not really in the mood for gaiety or festivities. The memory of the many who had died on the SS *Britannia* and probably in the other lifeboats was never very far from their thoughts.

Mary was relieved and delighted to receive two cables from Dr Maxwell. He had authorized a money order, so Mary had funds. He also told her of the contents of the cable (truncated as they always were) he had sent to Colin, which made her laugh: "Happy advise your wife safe arrival Montevideo."

"My husband is going to be completely bemused by this," she told the others. "He'll wonder what the devil I'm doing here. I'm supposed to be in Calcutta." With cash in her pocket she was immediately able to add to her meagre wardrobe.

On 14 April she said goodbye to Mrs Harrison and Miss Phelps. The local Methodist church that was organizing their repatriation to England took the missionaries under its wing. Mrs Harrison was obviously going to be without her husband for some time. Both she and Miss Phelps were comforted by the familiarity of the Methodist Mission. Suddenly Mrs Harrison was again bright and cheerful. She felt, she said, "at home". Mary kissed them goodbye with affection. There were promises of keeping in touch, which she was sure were unlikely to be kept. People, she knew, drifted in and out of each other's lives, even when their time together had been intense; others came to fill their place.

Saying goodbye to Ted Boddle, who was risking the Atlantic again to rejoin his regiment, was very different. She wept unashamedly. She hadn't been in love, but had become very fond of him. Their time together on the SS *Britannia* had been great fun. He was an amusing and likable companion. In the lifeboat she had clung to him both physically and emotionally and he had sustained and protected her with both robust and gentle support. On SS *Raranga* she discovered that he could be petulant and was easily irritated if she ever contradicted or challenged him, but they had shared so much in the most agonizing and perilous of situations that his departure was the severing of a link on which she had come to depend.

"How will I ever manage without you?"

He put his arms round her and held her close. "Don't leave me crying, Mary. You are braver and stronger than I am. Dry your eyes." He did so tenderly with his own handkerchief. "We've had an amazing time together. I will always remember you with affection and be proud to have known you."

She was very pleased he didn't make promises to keep in touch. She knew he would pass out of her life, like the missionaries, but the mark he left, like theirs, would be indelible.

At 9 p.m. on 14 April she took the night ferry to Buenos Aires. It was just over a month since she had left Liverpool. She felt a completely different person.

Interlude

In the spring of 1996 I took my mother to Walberswick in Suffolk, where we had two old-fashioned caravans on a small, pretty – if primitive – site, lying between the village and the beach. It was a favourite holiday destination of the family and I thought she would benefit from a change of scenery. The weather was very fine and extraordinarily she consented to sit outside in the evenings and to join the group of friends who congregated wherever the evening barbeque or drinks were taking place. She entranced them all. She was at her very best, vivacious, dynamic, and held court with what I can only call "aplomb".

"Isn't she wonderful?" I was told. "So sweet and interesting." She talked about India and our family life in Hong Kong with vivacity. She told anecdotes (some of which I had never heard before). A few were positively racy. One of the senior partners in the solicitors' office in Hong Kong where she worked as a secretary was a large and genial Chinese man. Every evening about 5 p.m. a beautiful Chinese girl arrived to wait for him to finish work. "Oh?" enquired my mother. "Is that his wife, come to make sure he goes straight home?"

"No," said my mother's boss. "That's his mistress come to make sure he *doesn't* go straight home." This story was greeted with howls of laughter and I saw her beaming with pleasure.

She was a great success. I saw her through other people's eyes.

Because we had two vans, she had her own bedroom and retired early, so we each got some personal space. The ten days passed pleasantly enough but I had to make as many concessions to her as I had to with the children in the past. She didn't like walking, hated the charming pub, and didn't want to come to the beach, so it was not a particularly restful holiday for me. A few years later, she expressed some surprise and even resentment that I had not repeated the experience. What I wanted to say was, "I love you dearly but you are such hard work!" I chose not to answer and she didn't persist.

Friends in Walberswick also expressed surprise that I hadn't brought my "delightful" mother with me on a second visit!

19

Buenos Aires: The Mysterious Monsieur Gué

15 APRIL

*M*ary felt very lost eating breakfast in the ferry's busy cafeteria. It was the first time she had been on her own since the evening in Liverpool at the Adelphi Hotel and she felt not a little scared and desolate. Once disembarked, feeling even more solitary and abandoned, she stood for a moment indecisively on the quay, looking for a taxi rank. She had noted the name of the hotel provided by the Embassy and had the paper clutched in her hand.

Glancing around, she saw a slim, pleasant-faced man (she guessed in his mid-fifties) approaching her. He was smiling. "Señora Stewart?" He took off his hat and bowed, smiling.

"Yes?"

"*Habla español?*"

"No, I'm afraid I don't speak Spanish."

"*O, Italiano?*"

"Not that either."

"*Parlez-vous français?*"

At last! "*Oui! Assez bien.*"

His face lit up, and from then on they spoke in French. "I've been sent to look after you," he told her. "My name is Fernand

Gué. I live here in the city." He took her suitcase and helplessly she followed him.

"By whom?" She got no answer to this, but as her gut feeling was that he wasn't a white slaver or a crook, she followed him to a taxi rank.

"I've been told to go to the Hotel des Immigres," she said. He looked shocked. "Oh, you can't possibly go there, my dear Madam; it's quite dreadful!"

He pointed it out to her from the taxi. It was a large ugly complex, used, Fernand Gué told her, to house the thousands of immigrants who flooded into Argentina during the Depression. She wondered why on earth it had been recommended: yet another mystery.

He took her instead to the Hotel Cinco Septiembre, a small elegant hotel built in the Spanish style. He swept her in and registered her before she could draw breath. He saw her to her room but made no effort to come in, which was a relief. Clearly neither a rapist nor a white slaver.

"My wife and I would be delighted if you would dine with us tonight," he said as he shook her hand and bowed. Bemused, Mary accepted. She realized she still didn't know who had organized this unexpected meeting and wondered if she might have missed a message left in the hotel in Montevideo.

She spent the morning resting, having slept badly on the ferry. In the afternoon she had a bath and went off as usual to find Thomas Cook. There was nothing for her. She was beginning to rely on the stream of messages from Dr Maxwell and was always disappointed and even resentful when there wasn't one, thinking they really ought to understand back home how much she relied on the contact. Disconsolately, she set out to do some shopping. Surprisingly, in the Calle Florida, an upmarket shopping street, she came across a branch of Harrods. To comfort herself, she went in, rashly she thought, and bought a frock.

As she was dressing for dinner, putting on her smart new frock, the reception desk phoned to say a gentleman was waiting for her downstairs. Imagining it was her mysterious new acquaintance, she finished her preparation and went down into the foyer. The "gentleman" was not Monsieur Gué, as she had expected, but a journalist and his photographer. She refused to speak to him, though he was very pressing and promised he would give a true and tasteful account of her adventures. Again, she refused and hurried into the bar. She felt cross and not a little alarmed. She wondered if Monsieur Gué had led the journalist to her.

When the latter arrived and Mary told him of the encounter, he became very angry and spoke rapidly in furious Spanish to the receptionist, who looked suitably contrite and embarrassed, and then apologized.

"They shouldn't have let him in," he said. "They could see what he was."

"Yes, but how did he know I was here?"

"Dear Madam, this is Buenos Aires. Nothing remains secret for long. Your arrival in Montevideo was in the papers. These bloodhounds sniff out the trail."

Monsieur Gué's home was beautiful: comfortable yet elegant with cream carpet and pale walls, flowers everywhere, and crystal glasses on the table. Mary was very pleased she had changed into her new outfit. Over dinner, his wife Sophie, a svelte and attractive blonde, revealed, "I have many friends in Montevideo. We knew that you would be here for over a week and thought you would like some family relaxation, some home comforts."

Yes, thought Mary, but how did they know she'd be there for that length of time?

Alone and friendless, her remaining time in Buenos Aires was spent with this charming, welcoming, sophisticated, and cultured French family. Despite her reservations and her misgivings, and recognizing that she was quite seduced by them, she decided that she would gain from the experience what she could and just be on her guard.

In their elegant home over magnificent food, wine, and whisky, and together with their daughter and her fiancé, they discussed music and literature, the theatre and modern art. The daughter played the violin exquisitely and her parents beamed at her with justifiable parental pride. They were devout Roman Catholics and said grace at every meal. They told her they attended Mass every day. Their devoutness and attachment to their religious faith and its practice brought back bittersweet memories of Michael.

In conversation, she was cautious. They never asked about the SS *Britannia,* or about the crew and the survivors. They did ask a great deal about England. Where did she live? What was it like in London? Were many people affected by the Blitz? Was there a lot of damage in the city? Which area was most affected? She fielded these apparently innocent and well-meant questions with dexterity. She down-played everything. No, she said, Dagenham was completely untouched. She thought wryly of the nightly air raids, the unpleasantness of trying to sleep in the shelter, and of the bombing. London was coping well with some damage, she told them, but morale was very high. This was true. The area around the docks was virtually unaffected, thanks to the barrage balloons! She smiled convincingly with her fingers metaphorically crossed and remembered with horror the appalling devastation. She had no idea whether they believed her or not. Neutral topics were easier: they asked about the Henley Regatta and the Epsom racecourse but she had been to neither. They thought the Royal Family quite wonderful and lamented that France was a republic.

One thing she did discover was that they were very pro-Vichy and thought Marshal Pétain, the "hero of Verdun", a wonderful example of French nationalism at its best. This, she thought, went with their Catholicism. They had no time at all for Charles de Gaulle, who they said was an arrogant man and a traitor to France. They were, Mary thought, snobbishly contemptuous of his "*petit bourgeois*" wife "Tante Yvonne", her lack of culture, and her appalling dress sense. Their wit was sharp, incisive, not particularly unkind but almost always apposite. To her shame, she remembered later, she often joined in their laughter and thought how easy it was to be sucked in to something that actually one deplored, merely because of the environment. Did not St Paul say, "Bad company corrupts good character"? Every night in her hotel bed she thought about them with pleasure at the evening of civilized and pleasant conversation, and yet with an underlying uncertainty.

Thomas Cook eventually got in touch. There was a cable from Dr Maxwell detailing her itinerary. She was to fly to San Francisco and sail across the Pacific to Bombay. Not unreasonably, they didn't want her to risk the Atlantic again.

The last weekend in Buenos Aires, the Gué family took her to the yacht club. They spent the afternoon rowing on the river and playing croquet on the lawn. It was a day of pure relaxation and pleasure. At face value, they were warm and friendly and irreproachable.

The expatriate community of English people there seemed to know the Gués, and greeted them with pleasure and a complete lack of reserve, despite their openly avowed attachment to Vichy France. Mary began to wonder, at that late date, if she had been foolish not to suspect that Fernand and Sophie had an ulterior motive in taking her on. She also considered that one of the questionable things about the English in Argentina was their relative indifference to what was happening elsewhere. Their life seemed one of pleasure and comfort, and they expressed no empathy at all with the deprivations and danger at home. They were untouched by the war.

On 24 April, the whole family came with her to the airport to see her off. Sophie Gué gave her a prayer book and a beautiful copy of *The Imitation of Christ*.

There were the usual promises to keep in touch, which Mary acknowledged politely. She knew she would never see them again: so ended her relationship with this charismatic and enigmatic family.

Interlude

One evening I had enticed my mother into the garden and, wrapped up warmly, she seemed content. As I had developed a taste for whisky she had lost hers, but she had discovered Stone's ginger wine and was happy and relaxed with a glass in one hand and a cigarette in the other. I wanted to pursue the topic of the mysterious Gué family.

"Surely it must have occurred to you that this strange family were at best fellow travellers and at worst Nazi spies. They just turned up out of the blue and sort of swept you up. Fernand said he had been sent to fetch you but you never established by whom. Did you ask again?"

"I didn't know what they were, that's true, and I am sure I would have been more careful under other circumstances. They were a complete mystery to me. But I was alone and friendless. For weeks I'd been in the eye of a storm and frankly I was only too glad to be taken under their wing. I would have been more worried if they had asked about the *Britannia* or even the *Raranga* but they didn't, and in the interests of national security I was discreet about life at home."

"You were more than discreet: you fed them disinformation, so you must have had your suspicions." She began to look troubled.

"Don't bully me! They were accepted everywhere. They were very kind to me. At that time, it was enough." I could tell she didn't really like being questioned too intensely about the Gués.

"I understand; it was all a long time ago; different times and difficult times. Tell me about Dotty, the girl on the plane."

20

Flight: A Cheerful New Zealander with a Novel Way of Paying Her Air Fare

*I*t took Mary eight days to reach San Francisco, country-hopping all the way, but it was another novel experience and she had always relished them.

The flight across the Andes was extraordinary. The view was spectacular. The jagged snowy peaks, not only white but blue and sometimes almost purple, thrilled and astonished her. The beauty of the terrain was unimaginable. She had never expected such variety. The summits, touched by the sun in the morning and evening, glimmered gold and vermillion like mountains on fire. She had moments of trepidation: the plane, so the pilot told them, was flying at 20,000 feet and Mary knew that several of the mountain peaks were nearly 23,000. She interpreted this as meaning that they would, on occasions, have peaks above them, flying, as it were, through valleys. She was relieved when it was announced that they would only fly during daylight hours.

A young woman who cheerfully introduced herself as "Daphne McAllister, known as 'Dotty'" took the seat next to Mary. "Dotty by name and I'm afraid dotty by nature." Mary took this clichéd statement in good part. She was a stout girl with a freckled face, a shock of red-gold hair and a pair of laughing hazel eyes. Mary warmed to her immediately.

"I should warn you," she told Mary, "I'm always bloody sick when we take off and land. They've given me extra bags and I am sure I'll need them. Once we are airborne, I'm OK." She was as good as her word and threw up with monotonous regularity. The stewardess did what she could, but it became evident that this was so frequent an occurrence that in the end she left her to it, providing her with extra sick bags, a large towel and a face cloth, which, between retching, Dotty thanked her for. She remained persistently cheerful. Mary was astonished at how rapidly this nausea resolved itself; she feared it would last until they reached cruising height but as soon as the plane began to climb, she recovered. Then it all happened again on descending. Curiously, Dotty was not in the least troubled by turbulence.

At each stop, all passengers and aircrew used the same hotel. Mary was happy to follow the crowd; she was much too tired to do anything else. In Santiago, while waiting to collect their luggage, Dotty, bursting with excitement, announced, "We are staying at the Crillon. This is really sweet!"

"What do you mean *really sweet?*"

"I mean it's the best. I know it's not France, but goodness, Mrs Stewart! I mean, the Crillon!"

The hotel was elegant and luxurious without being opulent. Mary was suitably impressed but, by now a seasoned traveller, was becoming quite blasé about all these "names".

An intimate friendly exchange over dinner that evening allowed Mary to ask this exuberant bubbly girl what her final destination was and whether she was travelling to a job.

The girl was not at all abashed, although she reddened. Charitably, Mary thought it could be the rum that she was drinking with such enthusiasm that coloured her cheeks.

"No, no," she said. "I haven't got a job to go to as such, although I may have to get one. I do get a job when I'm short of funds. I'm just hoofing it around the world. When I got on the plane at home I only had enough money for the first leg but I booked three stages. I got a job for a fortnight working on a farm."

She roared with laughter, throwing back her head and showing her pink healthy gums and strong white teeth. "My God, did I work, but I wanted to go on, so each stage if I hadn't got the readies I stayed for a bit, got a job and worked my passage. It was a bit like buying my ticket on the 'never-never', like hire purchase I guess." She stopped and bit her lip. "Sometimes money was easier to come by than at others." She leaned forward confidentially. "Men can be very generous, but I promise I never slept with anyone I didn't like."

Mary was stunned into silence by this astonishing revelation. Then she began to laugh and Dotty, relieved, began to laugh with her.

"You're not shocked?"

"No, not really. I suppose I ought to be shocked, but I've just faced a life or death experience so I expect it's made me more... well, tolerant. We live in strange times. 'The time is out of joint,' as Hamlet said. But what would your parents think?"

"I haven't got any parents, or if I have, I don't remember ever seeing them. I'm an orphan. I think there might be an uncle and aunt knocking about but I can't remember where. I've always had to make my own way. I wanted to travel; this was the only way I could do it."

"You could have saved up for the trip, of course." In Mary's world if you couldn't afford it, you couldn't have it. Dotty looked at her with silent scepticism. After a pause, she said, "I'd have been an old woman before I had enough for this adventure."

Later Mary was pleased she hadn't reproached the girl. Prostitution is not a very nice word but there was no avoiding it: sleeping with someone for money is precisely that; whether one likes them or not is completely irrelevant. Anyway, she thought, she was not responsible for her and all this dubious behaviour, and despite it all, Dotty was a kind and pleasant girl. She was an easy travelling companion and Mary wished her all the best. They parted ways at Guayaquil in Ecuador, Dotty saying vaguely that she thought she might have friends there. Mary was sorry to lose her company but pleased to have an empty seat beside her.

The towns and the stops began to flow into each other. The plane hopped all the way up South and Central America: Balboa, the Canal Zone, San José, Managua, Tegucigalpa, and San Salvador. On 30 April, they landed in Guatemala. The hotel was the shabbiest she stayed in. There was a broken light in her room and when it was fixed, to her irritation a swarm of insects flew in. A local production of Carmen kept her awake. It seemed to be happening immediately below her bedroom window. The toreador song was sung a second time, by popular request if the applause was any indication. She had always thought the song sounded like a man "shooting a line in a bar"! This was an opera that had never really appealed and on that hot sultry night it did so even less. Next morning she found herself covered with insect bites.

On and on they flew, sometimes short flights, sometimes longer. It was only her diary that kept a religious account of the timetable. She began to feel as if she had been travelling forever.

Interlude

I had to know what she meant by "shooting a line in a bar".

"Don't be silly!" She was recovering from a cold and was irritable. I had missed two evening sessions, having been away staying with a friend and she was sulky. "It means boastful, bragging, trying to impress."

I laughed. "These days when people talk about lines in bars, it usually refers to lines of cocaine."

She looked startled. "You youngsters," she said, and if she'd had enough hair, she would have tossed her head. "Cocaine's nothing new."

Then she began to sing a song. She didn't know all the verses but said it was well known in the thirties and often sung. The chorus went, "Honey, have a sniff, have a sniff on me. Honey, have a sniff on me!" I stared in astonishment. "Did you ever?"

"Gracious, no. I didn't move in that sort of circle. As to drugs, if you like, I was perfectly happy with my Craven A cigarettes. Nevertheless, cocaine was well known. Surely you don't think it's something new?" I stared in astonishment and she laughed aloud.

Over the years she changed to Silk Cut. She had a twenty-a-day habit, but if I had ever suggested she was addicted to nicotine, she would have been horrified. I never hear Carmen now without thinking of my mother, lines of cocaine, and other addictions.

Occasionally she came out with other incisive comments that made me laugh. Once we were discussing a TV programme about great painters, particularly Leonardo da Vinci.

"I love the lady with the stoat," she murmured.

"I think it's an ermine."

"Same animal. Don't they go white in winter? Anyway, she's beautiful. The girl, I mean."

"And what about the Mona Lisa?"

"Oh her!" she said almost with contempt. "Her, with her mysterious smile. I tell you what: that girl looks sly. I wouldn't trust her to hold my handbag."

It was so apt. If one looks closely she does look sly and is there a hint of a squint in that sideways glance? We both agreed that we thought the painting over-rated.

21

Los Angeles: Unpleasantness with Immigration

*M*ary arrived in Los Angeles on 2 May and was promptly detained by the American Immigration Department. Two officials, an older grim-looking, thickset man and a slim younger fellow, escorted her to a small room, sat her down behind a table and proceeded to interrogate her. Why had she come to the USA? Which countries had she passed through? Who had she been in contact with? Where had she come from, where was she going to, and for what reason? They seemed completely bemused by her statement that she was going to India. She might just as well have said she was going to Mars.

At first she answered all questions cheerfully, but eventually she became angered by their hostility. Her claim to be a British subject, supported by her British passport, should be enough, she said. At that point, they became positively aggressive. How, they wanted to know, had she, neither a British civil servant nor a member of the armed forces, obtained a passport in time of war?

"I work for an international pharmaceutical company. If you contact Dr Maxwell of May & Baker Ltd, he will vouch for me." This seemed to cut no ice with them. They huddled together for a moment, exchanging a whispered conversation, and then made to leave the room.

"Excuse me," Mary called. "I'd like a cup of tea, and if you are going to keep me here much longer, I would like the British Consulate informed!"

This seemed to have some effect. There was more whispering and then an assurance that they would bring a cup of tea. "Are you sure you wouldn't prefer coffee?" asked the younger man.

"Certainly not!" Mary replied. "And I'd like milk and no sugar!" She waited alone for about fifteen minutes and then the tea arrived, brought in by a timid looking young woman. Defiantly Mary lit a cigarette. "And I need an ashtray," she said.

After a further fifteen minutes, her two interrogators returned. To her dismay they repeated all their previous questions and compared the notes they had made. Finally, they rose, took her into another room and, despite her protests that she was neither an illegal immigrant nor a member of a hostile state, fingerprinted her.

"You are free to leave now," the older of the two officials said, dismissing her with a curt wave of his hand.

"Just a minute," said Mary. "I'll have my passport back, if you don't mind." They returned it to her with some reluctance. This involved further delay and signing of papers. She was instructed to report to the immigration authorities in San Francisco when she arrived there. When eventually she was released some six hours later, she felt entitled to a passing shot.

"You know," she declared, addressing the elder of her two hostile interrogators and tucking her passport away, "we could really do with you Americans helping us in Europe with the war effort, but if you are this scared about one English woman travelling alone, we are probably better off without you!" She had the satisfaction of seeing him look furious.

It was evening by the time she checked into the Clark Hotel. It was large, very comfortable, and very central downtown LA. Not for the first time she was grateful for the company to be taking such good care of her. All her accommodation had been satisfactory and some of it sumptuous. Her youth allowed her to cope with the stress of such constant travelling but she knew she had become very weary of living out of a suitcase. With five days to relax, she had the luxury of unpacking everything and putting her clothes in drawers and wardrobes. She had travelled 7,646 miles since being rescued by the SS *Raranga* and was more than a little tired of the constant displacement. She had an early dinner, a long luxurious bath, and fell into bed.

During her time in Buenos Aires she had met a pleasant Californian woman from Los Angeles, a declared Anglophile, who insisted that Mary contact her on her arrival in LA. This charming woman, Hilda Samson, responded with enthusiasm when Mary phoned her next morning, and arranged to meet her on 4 May, two days later.

The Thomas Cook office in LA had further tickets, an itinerary and, more importantly, a money order. It never occurred to Mary that this was money that she might have to pay back and she was correct in this: May & Baker assumed all her expenses. The British government was not so generous.

LA was so different from any English or Scottish town that initially she found it stark and lacking in character. The grid system of the street layout was certainly practical but it was featureless. She was accustomed to the higgledy piggledy unplanned towns at home that had grown up over hundreds of years, with their twisting haphazard lanes, unexpected turnings, narrow pavement-less roads and dead ends. Used to Tudor, Georgian, and Victorian architecture, she searched in vain for old buildings or for distinguished monuments. Everything looked brash and new. However, after a day sightseeing and shopping, the city won her over. The straight roads and clear perspective made finding one's way around very easy, and when she went further afield and took the funicular from the Angel Flight gateway up to Bunkers Hill, she found a delightful mixture of fine nineteenth-century houses and art deco facades. The people, above all, were friendly and helpful, and as usual intrigued by her soft Scottish accent. The weather was fine and sunny. So she relaxed, found people to chat to, and began to enjoy herself.

Hilda Samson came to collect her as promised on the 4th and undertook to show her some local sights. She was a tall, loud, friendly woman, clearly determined that Mary should see everything that LA had to offer. She drove a large Packard with immense dash. She talked all the time, pointing out things and places of interest. "That's the Hollywood Bowl. It's a concert hall; I think it was designed by Frank Lloyd Wright. He's real famous. Do you see that oriental building? That's the TCL Chinese Theatre. I've never been inside but they say it's marvellous. I really ought to take you to Beverley Hills; Rodeo Drive has such wonderful shops!"

Hilda had an alarming habit of taking her eyes off the road and her hands off the steering wheel in order to gesture at these noteworthy buildings or monuments. Noticing Mary flinch as she took a corner at speed and well over to the other side of the road, she said bracingly, "I hope you're not scared, honey. I always drive like this and ain't had a smash yet." She swung the wheel violently to avoid a lorry coming towards them: "Ah, these darn trucks; they're everywhere these days."

"Don't you need to stay on your side of the road?" asked Mary, hanging on to the sides of her seat. She tried not to be too worried by what she thought was reckless driving. Having survived death in the Atlantic, she sincerely hoped she would not face it again within sight of the Pacific.

They went out to Santa Monica, which Hilda said was more interesting than Long Beach. This beautiful suburb enchanted Mary: the beachfront, the golden sands, the gorgeous houses. It was clearly very affluent; both the men and the women were elegant and well-dressed. She and Hilda sat outside a beach café under palm trees and ate ice cream with fudge sauce, which

Hilda assured her was an American speciality. "Do you have anything like this at home?" she enquired.

"Well, we do have ice cream! But in fairness it's not as good as this. Dunoon, my home town, has quite a pleasant beach too... " She laughed as she spoke. "But no palm trees, and although it is supposed to have a micro-climate, it is rarely this warm." She was suddenly filled with a strange nostalgia and felt a long, long way from home.

Later they strolled along the pier but the amusement arcade was not to Mary's taste, which Hilda recognized, so she drove back to the hotel and came into the bar for an evening drink, saying mysteriously, "I've got a treat for you tomorrow! I'll pick you up at noon."

22

A Chance Encounter with the "Great Dictator" and the "Dook"

"I'm taking you to Hollywood," announced Hilda. "You can't come to LA and not visit Hollywood." She suddenly hesitated and looked uncertain. "You do have movies at home, don't you?" Having learned in the course of conversation the previous day that few people had fridges and almost nobody a telephone in their house, she was clearly beginning to think of life in the UK as very primitive.

"Yes," replied Mary, very straight-faced, "we do have movies, though not drive-in ones."

Hilda looked uncertain, not sure if she was being teased. "Anyway," she said, "that's by the by. Have you ever heard of The Brown Derby?"

"No, I haven't; is it a clothes store?"

Hilda laughed. "No, it isn't! It's a very famous restaurant patronized by the stars. I'm taking you there for lunch. There are a couple of Brown Derby restaurants in LA but this is the best one! It's situated on Hollywood and Vine, and very near the film studios."

The interior of the restaurant was charmingly, if eccentrically, decorated. Every table was lit by a lamp, and the shades were all brown bowler hats! Hilda told Mary that the other Brown Derby restaurant was actually shaped like a bowler.

The place was busy but as Hilda had booked, they were shown swiftly to a table. They sat in an alcove. Mary looked about keenly. There were a number of very heavily made-up men and women at the bar and at table. "Probably starlets or extras," Hilda told her. "They've come straight off set and may be needed again this afternoon."

The place had a buzz about it that Mary found exhilarating, but after about ten minutes when nobody notable had arrived, Hilda resigned herself to the prosaic business of ordering food. They both had the cobb salad, the house speciality, and then ordered coffee. Just as Mary was lighting up, two men, who had apparently been seated at the alcove behind them, stopped at their table. One was small with dark wavy hair, the other very tall, with what Mary thought of as a craggy face – pleasant enough, but irregularly featured. They both smiled. The older man bowed slightly and leaned forward enquiringly.

"Was that a Scottish accent I overheard?"

As soon as he spoke, she recognized him and shivered with excitement.

"Yes it was, Mr Chaplin. I'm a Glaswegian." Then remembering her companion quivering beside her, Mary said, "This is my friend Mrs Samson; she lives here but I am just passing through."

Both men nodded politely. Chaplin continued, "You know, I'm a Londoner myself and although my home is here I still feel English at heart. It's always good to hear an accent from home."

Glasgow, Mary thought, was a long way from London but she didn't say so.

His voice was agreeable, with a slight American modulation. "I am often in London and Londoners are very kind and welcoming to me."

"I'm pleased," Mary replied. "You've given a lot of people a great deal of pleasure and I must tell you, *The Great Dictator* was wonderful!"

He bowed again. "Thank you. It was a big departure for me: my first venture into the 'talkies'. It's been charming to talk to you. Give London my best when you are next there." Then he gave a sudden exclamation: "Forgive me, I am forgetting my manners. This handsome young fellow is Mr John Wayne; he's going to be big, very big indeed."

Mr John Wayne looked bashful and said, "Oh, I don't know about that!"

This affable and easy-going young man rejoiced in the nickname "Duke", pronounced by Americans, Mary learned later, as "Dook" – something which for years afterwards made her laugh. He'd had this nickname from childhood.

"Have you seen *Stagecoach*?" asked Chaplin. Mary hadn't, but she didn't think it polite to say so.

"I've seen it twice," interjected Hilda. "I loved it!" Chaplin smiled but turned back to Mary.

"It's been a real pleasure talking to you, Mrs...?"

"Stewart, Mary Stewart."

"A very proper Scottish name, Mrs Mary Stewart." She stood up and he took her hand and shook it, nodding to Hilda. Mary found John Wayne towering above her. He too shook her hand, saying in a slow grave voice, "You take care now, l'il lady."

She and Hilda stared at the retreating forms. When they had gathered their wits, they realized that every head in the restaurant was turned toward them.

"Well!" said Hilda. "I can't believe it. And you recognized him?"

"Charlie Chaplin? Yes, of course, but not the other one."

"You heard what Mr Chaplin said – he's going to be big – I mean famous! Actually, I thought *Stagecoach* was poor but others must have liked it."

Mary said goodbye to Hilda at the hotel. Again, there were profuse intentions of staying in touch, and addresses were exchanged, but Mary knew this was another acquaintance that would be lost in time. She was very grateful and pleased to have spent two days with such an agreeable companion, but it was with some relief that she found herself alone again.

Interlude

My mother told me this story in the car one day when I was taking her back to Hove to visit a friend. This extraordinary account, which was not on the tapes, stunned me. What could I do? Accuse her of making it up? But she was so vehement in her insistence that it was true that I had to accept it. She was also outraged that I was inclined to be sceptical.

"We went," she pointed out, "to a restaurant patronized every day by people from the film world. If you went to Stratford-upon-Avon and drank in a pub where all the company went for a drink, don't you think you might have bumped into some of the famous actors? Look, at the Old Cross in Chichester you were always meeting the glitterati. Anyway," she added, "it's a myth that actors are shy and retiring, yearning for an ordinary life. They love being recognized. It's honey to their tongue, meat and drink to them."

I had to laugh, believing this at least to be true.

"Did you like him?"

"He was charming, obviously, even flirtatious. Yes, he seemed pleasant. But you know, in a five-minute meeting it's difficult to get a true impression."

In the course of our daily interaction, I had come to realize how she reacted to masculine charm. Her boss Mr Choppin, Dr Maxwell, Ted Boddle, Captain Starr, Monsieur Gué, and now this famous actor–director: an element of coquetry underpinned all her interactions with men. She was always a little arch, a little flirtatious. It was not unattractive but it explained her view of men and how they reacted to her.

23

The Angelus Temple: An Odd Experience

*M*ary felt she couldn't leave LA without at least seeing the Angelus Temple where the "red-hot gospeller" Aimee Semple McPherson held her revivalist meetings. In the event, when the taxi driver dropped her off in front of the huge domed building, Mary discovered she was just in time for an evening session. The taxi driver offered to pick her up afterwards.

Inside, the auditorium was vast. Mary learned later that it could hold nearly 5,000 people. It was, she thought, more like a theatre or concert hall than a church. There was a stage rather than a choir or sanctuary, and the seats were tiered. The whole place was magnificently decorated with huge banks of flowers. The temple filled quickly and Mary found herself swept to the front, where she would have a good view of the proceedings. She looked in vain for a pulpit or an altar; there was certainly no sign of a cross or indeed any Christian symbol.

The choir was magnificent, their robes shimmering and their singing she thought sublime. However, that was the high point. On stage, a man asleep on a bed was supposed to represent a church asleep that Aimee was to bring to life. Her arrival was greeted with rapturous applause. She was a good-looking blonde in her early fifties and the service, such as it was, clearly roused an enthusiastic response. Mary thought the spiritual content was thin. Faith, she felt uneasily, was not all hallelujah, hallelujah. When the performance ended – she couldn't bring herself to call it a service – people began to crowd toward the stage. She found herself carried along with them until she was standing directly in front of the evangelist. Hands were placed on her head.

Aimee spoke. "You have suffered some, and passed through difficult times but you go forward in the light of the Lord."

"Thank you," said Mary and then feeling this was somewhat inadequate, repeated, "Thank you very much." Later it occurred to her that this anodyne "blessing", if that was what it was, showed no uncanny knowledge of Mary's recent adventure but could apply to almost anyone. Who hasn't come through troublesome times?

"Well?" enquired the taxi driver. "What did you make of her?"

She didn't want to be rude, so said carefully, "It was very interesting."

"It ain't my kind of religion, lady," was the succinct response.

Interlude

"I suppose she was the Billy Graham of her day. I've never heard of her." My comment about Sister Aimee, as she was called, was not critical, just matter of fact. My mother, rather testily, pointed out that most people in the 1990s, certainly those under twenty-five, had never heard of Billy Graham either.

I thought a great deal about my mother attending this odd event but after talking at some length about it to her, decided that alternative forms of religion intrigued her, and this would have accounted for her desire to hear the celebrated preacher. I knew she had once gone to a spiritualist meeting in Southsea, despite, in later life, having become a practising Catholic. Deep down, the theatricality of this sort of thing appealed to her. In the years I spent talking to her, I was often struck by how emotionally charged her language was. She disliked cliché but her delivery was often dramatic, her voice becoming filled with a kind of vibrato when she was moved by something. Occasionally I teased her and she would get cross, but usually ended up laughing; she knew it was true.

"Did you just go out of curiosity or did you think you might get something spiritual out of it?" I was keen to probe what had been her true reason for attending such a glitzy form of worship, and looked to have my suspicions about her enjoyment of alternative religious worship confirmed, but they weren't.

She insisted that it was curiosity alone that took her there. "She was very famous. I mean internationally famous. Her church was fabulously wealthy and she was really a media celebrity. All her shows or services were broadcast. But she did a great deal of good too. I believe, during the Depression, the Angelus Temple ran soup kitchens and she opposed the colour bar and other forms of discrimination." She laughed. "The Americans are very enthusiastic about Christian revivalism; they take religion in general very seriously indeed."

"You take your religion very seriously too! After all, you converted to Catholicism from Presbyterianism; some departure," I teased her. "I would have thought Sister Aimee of the Angelus meeting was right up your street!"

She denied it heatedly, looking shocked. "Oh no! That's not my type of thing at all. All that splendour and showy presentation. I prefer my church to be an altogether more sober affair."

"Well," I said, "you can't accuse the Catholic church of being lacking in excess. Look at Rome – all that amazing opulence in the Vatican and the quasi-hero worship of the Pope. What about the processions and the great feast days; the smells and bells; the flocking to somewhat dubious sites of pilgrimage?"

"It's not the same thing at all! With the church, it is tradition. It stretches back 2,000 years. It's like the monarchy: it's not personal glorification."

"You try telling that to the Archbishop of Westminster or to any Curia Cardinal! Princes of the church – that's what they call themselves, and they dress and live accordingly. Not much Christ-like poverty and simplicity there."

She stomped off crossly to make tea, and we returned later to her journey.

"Further adventures of Mary Stewart," I said, and she lit another cigarette.

24

San Francisco: Bagels and "Twittering"

With some difficulty, Mary located the Customs and Immigration offices and presented herself in San Francisco as she had been directed. She could hear music coming through the closed door and had to knock twice before it was opened. She was apprehensive. But she had no need to worry.

"Come right on in." The two cheerful and chubby immigration officers welcomed Mary with surprising and unconcealed enthusiasm. "Have a chair, ma'am."

She had been prepared for a repetition of the aggressive and menacing behaviour of their counterparts in LA, and this was a pleasant surprise. There were plants on the windowsill and a large black and white dog of indeterminate breed under a desk, which raised its head, looked at Mary, yawned, and returned to its slumber.

"And what brings you to us?" These two were clearly puzzled as to the purpose of her visit. But they were welcoming and drew out a chair for her. Mary sat down.

"Didn't you get a phone call or a message from Immigration in Los Angeles? They said it was vital to report to you and that they would get in touch with you and send my papers to this office."

The two officials looked at each other then slowly shook their heads. They did this in unison, and then announced slowly, with one voice. "No, we've had nothing from those guys." Mary had a strong desire to laugh. Their rotund physique swelled their navy-blue uniforms; every button was doing its duty. They were so similar in shape and height they could have been brothers, and she thought irresistibly of Tweedledum and Tweedledee.

"Well," said Tweedledum sighing, "I s'pose we ought to fill in the paperwork." He began to rummage disconsolately among the files scattered on his desk.

"Nah," said Tweedledee, easing his trousers and running his hand over a bald and shining head. "This young lady doesn't look like any threat to Uncle Sam. Paperwork just causes problems. We'll just make a note in today's report so they can't say she didn't report in. What d'ya say?" They both stared seriously at her. She wondered if they were waiting for her to make the decision. Tweedledum fidgeted and was clearly not reassured by his partner's suggestion. Suddenly he brightened, and addressing his colleague, he said, "We *will* do the paperwork and since you're not so keen, I'll do it, and you go fetch us some coffee and bagels!"

The time spent on the paperwork was considerably shortened by excellent coffee and, for Mary, the novel experience of bagels, cream cheese, and what she was told was "lox". She thought it was smoked salmon but they assured her earnestly that it wasn't smoked salmon but brined salmon. "It's a whole different thing, ma'am." She found the bagel chewy but full of flavour. It was delicious.

She spent a couple of hours in the office. They seemed curiously reluctant to let her go, introducing new topics of conversation just as she was on the point of leaving. They showed her photos of their wives and children, of their pets, and of what they called "the yard", which Mary was surprised to find was in fact the garden.

They were astonished and disappointed that she had no photos of her own on her. They told her they had never met "a real English lady" before and were full of apologies when she told them she was Scottish, wondering anxiously if they had offended her! It took a lot of reassurance to calm them. She began to suspect that they were bored and had welcomed her arrival as a means of alleviating the tedium of their daily and clearly uneventful life. They told her they had very little work and days could pass without any "aliens" coming through. Once again, addresses were exchanged without any real expectation, on either side, of renewed acquaintance. She thought it strange how difficult people sometimes found it just to say goodbye. You can't stay friends with everybody you meet, she reasoned.

She was booked into the Mark Hopkins, another elegant and sophisticated hotel. Her bedroom had a faintly Caledonian theme with attractive prints of what looked like Highland scenes and some tartan cushions on the plump red sofa. Despite the total dissimilarity, it called to mind the Argyll Hotel in Dunoon: both establishments had an air of supreme self-confidence, the one dominating Nob Hill, a particularly evocative name, Mary thought, and the other boldly present at the end of the esplanade. Taking a long and luxurious soak in water foaming with perfumed bath oil, she found herself humming ironically the post-World War I song that she had learned from her brothers: "How ya going to keep 'em down on the farm after they've seen Paree?" Dunoon and its associations seemed a million miles away.

The Mark Hopkins was the last in a line of beautiful hotels that she could never have afforded had she been paying for them herself. Who had chosen them and who continued to send regular and generous money orders via Thomas Cook, she wondered? Was it the company or Dr Maxwell? She suspected the latter.

She spent her final day in San Francisco in an orgy of shopping at Magnin's department store (now Macy's). Ahead of her was a six-week sea voyage and in preparation for and anticipation of it, she bought a completely new wardrobe, from underwear to evening dresses. May & Baker had sent a money order for $500.

Normally careful with money, even frugal, she felt wildly and guiltily extravagant. The store offered to deliver her parcels to her hotel. She was always impressed by the wonderful service that was available in America. In England, all commercial exchanges were characterized by diffidence and hesitation on the one hand, and bored semi-resentment on the other. Mary remembered exchanges along the lines of:

"I wonder, do you perhaps have it in another colour?"

"No, this is all we've got. Will that be all, Madam?"

Here they were keen and pleased to serve, and above all polite. Unencumbered by her purchases, she spent the evening exploring further afield.

On the recommendation of Tweedledum and Tweedledee she visited the Chinese Telephone Exchange. Outside the three-tiered pagoda building a stately mandarin in Chinese dress bowed her in. She passed through one or two beautifully decorated ante-rooms, where deliciously refreshing green tea and cigarettes were graciously offered. She accepted them with, she hoped, equal grace. The telephone room itself was decorated with gold and red banners, and tasselled lanterns hung from the ceiling. Women, all young and all pretty, operated the switchboards. They wore the traditional cheongsam dress in a variety of colours, tightly fitted to their petite and slender shape. The dress was high-collared with a slit to the thigh. Mary thought she had never seen such a beautiful collection of girls. A middle-aged woman, who introduced herself as a "chaperone", explained that all the girls spoke perfect English and at least five Chinese dialects. They had to memorize the names of all the subscribers, their addresses, and occupations – nearly 4,000 of them.

"In China," the chaperone explained, "it is rude to call people by a number, so a caller would say, 'Please put me through to Mrs Nancy Wong in such and such a building,' and the operator will know the number and connect the caller. We get over a thousand calls a day," she added with a smile.

Mary found it both extraordinary and exotic. The voices of the telephone operators reminded her of birds twittering and cooing. As she left, they bowed and smiled. She was quite enchanted. Stepping out into the hot and busy street, she felt she had passed from one century into another.

On 9 May, over two months after leaving Liverpool, she travelled down to the docks complete with new luggage, and embarked on the white and gleaming SS *President Monroe*, preparing to sail on another world cruise.

25

Another Ship, Another Ocean

The cabin was not as opulent as the Mark Hopkins Hotel but compared to the poor lost SS *Britannia*, it was luxurious. The steward who brought up her luggage referred to it as a stateroom. Mary felt she had become quite accustomed to a certain comfort but her only experience of sailing had been a small, shared cabin and a narrow hard bunk. Here she had a large bed, a window rather than a porthole, and, best of all, her own bathroom. She unpacked her clothes and laid her hairbrush, comb, and mirror on the dressing table, remembering, with a pang, her lovely dressing case, now on the floor of the Atlantic. She bounced experimentally on the bed and discovered a good thick mattress and beautiful linen sheets.

The ship was due to sail at 3 p.m. so she went up on deck to join other passengers thronging the rails. She was surprised how few of them there were. The SS *President Monroe* was not a huge ship. Mary saw from the manifest pinned up outside the purser's office that although there was room for ninety-five passengers, all first class, fewer than forty had embarked. She noticed with amusement more missionaries, and thought the world was full of globe-trotting Christians, all carrying the word of the Lord to the heathen. Then she felt ashamed of mocking, even in her thoughts, such good people, thinking of Mrs Harrison and Miss Phelps. She wondered what had become of them.

A steward arrived with a basket and handed out spools of coloured paper that the passengers launched to their friends and relatives on the quayside as the ship drew away. There were shouts of "aloha". Mary didn't have anyone to shout "aloha" to, but she shouted anyway and tossed her coloured spools with happy abandon.

In the bar, a large welcoming space, she introduced herself to several people but felt with some dismay that they seemed moderately dull. A ponderous German executive and his stout *hausfrau* of a wife she ignored out of principle. She overheard them say that they had moved to the United States in the thirties. From their manner and appearance, she thought very little of the American way of life had rubbed off on them. They seemed rigidly Prussian. The missionaries were pleasant but quiet. A plump young Middle Eastern man introduced himself by announcing, "I am Sheikh Ali Khalifa bin Ali Al [as my mother pronounced it] from Bahrain and you are cute!" *I will certainly avoid him*, Mary thought. There were two other couples: one very shy – on their honeymoon, they confided, blushing. There was another older pair, garrulous beyond belief, who said this was their third world cruise. Without any reticence, they began to voice their opinion about cruising in general and the boat in particular.

"We've been on the *President Hoover* and this is quite small in comparison. There are only about thirty passengers so far, but I guess more will come each time we arrive at a different port. The Japs are OK, but avoid the Koreans. And I wouldn't share the pool with a Malay."

Stunned by the shameless racism of the remark, even in a country where colour prejudice was alive and well, Mary began to wish she had stayed in her cabin. She went to the bar to get a drink and to distance herself from such unpleasant company, when, next minute, the door opened and about six men entered. Laughing and talking they swarmed toward the bar. They were an exuberant bunch who immediately fell into conversation with Mary in the relaxed and friendly manner she had come to recognize as quintessentially American. They were American naval officers en route for Singapore. She liked them all straight away. They addressed her as "ma'am" but by the end of the first evening they were on first name terms.

Two of them were at her table at dinner, together with the second purser, Mr Hetherington. One of the officers in particular appealed to Mary. He was quiet, tall, slim, and fair-haired. Mary thought he had a Scandinavian look about him. This was confirmed when he said his mother was Swedish. His name was Christian Gulliver; his companions called him "Gully". Mary never called him anything other than Gully.

They all loved her accent and sometimes asked her to repeat words in order to laugh at them again. For some reason they thought "blimey" was hilarious. It was an exclamation she often used; one she had picked up from her husband. For the life of her, she could not think why they found it so amusing. They were delighted with the story of her meeting Charlie Chaplin but were disappointed it wasn't Bob Hope: "Yeah, Chaplin's OK, but Bob Hope, now he's the greatest."

They were extraordinarily impressed about her going to the Angelus Temple to hear Aimee Semple McPherson, whom they praised as a good Christian and an example to "the godless", but they spoke laughingly and Mary had the feeling that, despite all this, their religious belief sat lightly on their shoulders.

At the end of that first day she went to bed happy and sure that a long and interesting voyage lay ahead. She thought about Gully, the quiet one, and his dry humour. As she had left the bar, Sheikh Ali had approached and stroked and pressed her arm; she had instinctively shrunk away. Gully had drawn her to his other side. "Push off, pal," he said tersely. "Ignore him, Mary," he reassured her. "He's been very expensively educated in all the best bars and brothels in San Francisco."

She fell asleep with Gully's voice in her ear and the memory of his protective arm around her.

After leaving San Francisco, the weather was rough and continued to be so until they reached Honolulu. The ship claimed to have stabilizers, but Mary was almost thrown from her bed one night. The foghorn sounded continuously. She hoped fervently that they were not going to be dogged by bad weather for the entire voyage.

Few people appeared in the dining room. The American officers were cheerfully unaffected and after a queasy twelve hours Mary too was fine. During the day she joined them happily in the bar where they welcomed her with ease and evident pleasure. They played gin rummy and *vingt-et-un* for matchsticks. One evening they produced a game called Chinese chequers, which could be played by two or more people; she became rapidly addicted.

The beauty and elegance of the ship continued to delight her – not just the comfortable stateroom but also the lounges, the bar, the understated, sophisticated dining room, the promenade deck, and above all the swimming pool. Her naval friends were less than complimentary.

"Her appearance is all very well," said Gully, "but she's a mean ship. That's why she rolls like a cow, even with stabilizers: too much superstructure."

He tried to explain to Mary how to wrap herself into her sheet to stop herself from falling out of bed, and to anchor the ends under the mattress, but it all sounded too complicated, so she just tucked herself in more securely and eventually the seas abated.

Occasionally, despite the good company and feeling increasingly drawn to Gully, she sensed herself to be deeply alone. Once she had left Montevideo and her companion castaways, there was no one with whom she could share that life-changing experience. She had not talked about it to anyone, except in the most casual manner. Furthermore, she saw clearly that those not involved in it preferred not to talk about a foreign conflict. In fact, she herself, so far from home, was beginning to feel almost detached from war-ravished Europe. It was as if those terrible events were happening in another world. In her current one, it was all light and laughter, frivolity, and indeed indifference, so when, on 12 May, Gully came to find her to tell her that Rudolf Hess had flown to Scotland on a "peace mission" she stared at him in open-mouthed astonishment.

"Rudolf Hess, Hitler's deputy? It's unbelievable. Can you tell me anything more?" she asked.

"Sorry," he said wryly. "That's all I know. It happened on the 10th May apparently. It's written up on the daily bulletin outside the purser's office."

"What can it mean? Is it really a peace initiative? Hitler's a madman; he would never agree to this." She looked around the dining room, expecting this news to set the place on fire, but it was met with virtual indifference. Gully consoled her, "They don't know about Europe, Mary; the war is happening elsewhere." Then he added, "But maybe not for long." She didn't know whether to be comforted or dismayed by this. There was no further information and the purser was sympathetic but unable to be helpful, promising that if he heard more, he would tell her. As she was deliberately not on speaking terms with the German couple, she couldn't ask them their view, although she was tempted. She felt restless all day.

The next morning, when they docked in Honolulu, Gully came to knock on her door. The weather was sunny.

"Come on," he said. "The fellows are going ashore. We'll get some lunch and see the town a bit; you need to clear your head."

Reluctantly she allowed herself to be persuaded and eventually, more cheerfully, joined them, and then felt herself to be quite dashing, going ashore with six very personable young men. They all took a taxi from the docks. Some of them went to the beach, but she and Gully wandered around the town and lunched at a seafood restaurant. Teasingly, he tried to introduce her to rum and Coke but she shook her head, laughed, and drank delicious fresh pineapple juice instead. Later in the evening they sat on the warm sand and in silence listened, happy and relaxed, to the breakers crashing on the shore.

She reflected, "I should be afraid of the sea – it so nearly did for me – but I love it. I relish its endless variety, its power, its dominance, and yet its indifference to us. We have no control over it. We are all King Canute when we face the tide. It only obeys the moon. It demands total respect, doesn't it?"

She watched the waves running softly up the beach towards them and then retreating with a hiss and a sigh. "This Pacific seems a gentler ocean than the tough Atlantic, more female somehow; not weaker but subtler."

"You are such a romantic, Mary. You haven't seen the Pacific in a real storm. Have you forgotten how it nearly threw you out of bed?" And so, laughing and chatting, arm in arm, they returned to the ship late in the evening, garlanded with lei. The next day, they sailed for Kobe, Japan.

The weather became much warmer and Mary and her companions spent hours by the swimming pool lying on the steamer chairs, which were surprisingly comfortable, despite being made of wood. Her friends called this time R & R – rest and relaxation – and only left the pool to go to the bar. She smiled at them and ordered fresh lemonade when they offered to fetch her a drink. She chatted and read and snoozed and swam. In the afternoon, under shady umbrellas, she wrote her diary. She was very circumspect over what she wrote about Gully but she knew that their attraction was mutual. With surprising delicacy, his companions teased neither of them, although their increasing intimacy was very evident.

Interlude

My mother very slowly revealed to me the story of her wonderful romantic trip. The tapes were factual but it was in her conversation that I discovered the nature of that fairy-tale voyage. It was a shipboard romance, as intense and all-encompassing as it was fleeting.

She described everything: her cabin, her table companions, other passengers, the fancy dress ball, and the parties around the pool. The name "Gully" seemed to figure regularly in her narrative.

"Come on, then." I said "Tell me about Gully. Were you in love?"

She laughed: "Oh yes, of course I was." She was smiling and her face was soft and tender as if her memories were very sweet. "Are you shocked?"

"No, not at all; it was so long ago. Was it a real affair?"

"Not straight away. It's silly but I wanted the romantic side of it first of all. I wanted to be wooed, not seduced. Although," she laughed again, "in fact it was me, really, who did the seducing. I suppose you could say I was shameless."

"What about Colin? Did you think of him? Did you feel guilty?"

"Colin? Colin was in another world, a parallel world if you like. If I hadn't had his photograph, I don't think I could even have remembered his face."

I found this hard to take in. My father was one of the most memorable individuals I ever knew. His personality was large. He was dynamic, even seductive; people didn't forget Colin. "You must have been very smitten."

"Yes, but I knew it was so ephemeral. *Carpe diem*, as they say, and so I did. I gave myself up to it completely, knowing how brief it would be. We were in a bubble." She often used this expression when she wanted to describe her detachment from reality.

Her revelations raised questions in me that I had wanted to ask for a very long time.

"Tell me something. When I was a teenager and even when I left the religious life, why were you so dishonest with me about boyfriends? Why did you insist about things that from personal experience you knew to be untrue?"

She looked startled and said, "Whatever do you mean?" But I knew by her evasive expression and her blush that she knew what was coming.

"Well, it's all water under the bridge now. I'm a happily married woman and mother of two children. But what was all this, no man wants... What was the expression? 'Shop-soiled goods'? And, 'He'll never marry you if he's had his wicked way with you.' 'He'll lose all respect for you.' Clearly, it was untrue in the forties and in the sixties and even less true in the seventies. From your own experience, you must have known it was false. Did my father lose all respect for you? Did Gully? Why weren't you honest with me?"

"Oh, for goodness' sake!" she expostulated. "What mother is going to admit to her own follies? Anyway, it's what all mothers say to their daughters!"

"Is it?" I said. "Is it really?"

"Naturally it is! They want to protect them."

"In that case," I said sharply, "you'd have done better to have whisked me smartly along to the doctor to get me the pill."

She looked stricken. "I never thought of that! It wasn't so easy to get hold of the pill in the early sixties and I didn't know for certain the nature of your relationship with boyfriends. Anyway, you went into a convent for heaven's sake! I can't think of any mother who would have done what you suggest. The truth of the matter is, I probably didn't want to know!" She was close to tears.

I felt an odd mixture of shame and irritation. She frequently generated this sort of emotion in me. I thought of her courage in the lifeboat, followed by her long solitary journey. A little shipboard romance didn't seem too reprehensible in the light of that life-changing experience. But why was there one code of behaviour for her and another for me?

I went in to see her before going to bed. She was making a cup of tea, her Parkinson's more marked than usual, perhaps due to our conversation earlier. So I filled her cup and sat in companionable silence with her for a moment. She had obviously been thinking about what I had said.

"I wanted to be a good mother," she said plaintively. "I just don't think I was very good at it." I knew that what she was looking for was reassurance. *She's an old woman,* I thought, *and it was a very long time ago. I don't have the right to trouble her memories or to make her feel guilty.*

"Mummy, you were fine. You were loving. We shared holidays. We laughed a lot and even bought hats together." This was a reminder of a promise she had made me when I was a very little girl: "When you grow up we'll go shopping and buy hats." We had realized the promise the year before I went to France to enter the noviciate. I wondered fleetingly what had happened to the hat.

So I didn't speak of the times when I thought she had been a less than satisfactory parent, when she had self-indulgently unburdened herself to me when I was just an adolescent and vulnerable: telling me things I would really have preferred not to know about – my father's infidelity, or her financial worries, both of which frightened me.

The difference in her behaviour when she was with others – my brother, my husband, my in-laws, her carers – outgoing, cheerful and relaxed, compared to her self-obsession when she was with me, was hard to accept. I thought of her selfishness about my wedding, making it impossible for me to invite my father. I knew he had treated her cruelly, so she had some excuse, but it had pained me and outraged John.

I knew I was going to have to suppress many challenging questions if I wanted to hear the rest of her story in detail.

26

King Neptune's Court
and Tragic News

"Tomorrow," Gully told her, "we're crossing the line."

"Whatever do you mean? We aren't anywhere near the equator," said Mary, puzzled.

Gully laughed. "The International Date Line, not the equator. We sail into another time zone and lose a day. There will be a great party – fun and games – it's traditional. Anybody who's not crossed before will be initiated and will appear before King Neptune, so keep your swimsuit close by. The captain's crossed at least twice but the purser and the head steward are 'slimy pollywogs'. That means they've never done it, so they'll have to face King Neptune and pay a forfeit."

"What about you lot?" asked Mary, intrigued.

"Some of us are 'shellbacks'. That means we have crossed. But there are one or two who haven't, and they'll be for the high jump. And with a bit of luck, so will Sheikh whatshisname, and our know-it-all businessman."

The 18 May was a day of riotous activity. The captain, dressed as King Neptune, presided over a court of pirates and water nymphs, who raced up and down the deck covering people, passengers, and crew alike with shaving foam, flour, and water and sawdust. The indignities were in the main reserved for the men, and most entered into the spirit of the day with gusto. Clothes had to be put on inside out and backwards. Large tubes, coated with grease, were set up and people had to wriggle through them. Raw eggs were produced and those who couldn't eat them had them smeared over their heads. Finally, a board was stretched across the pool and those to be initiated were pushed onto it and unceremoniously tipped into the water. Women were not excused from this event. Mary, having been forewarned, had put on her swimsuit immediately after breakfast but others were tipped into the water fully dressed. With grim satisfaction, Mary watched the German couple unceremoniously dunked. When the ceremony was over, they were all awarded a certificate saying they were now shellbacks.

In the evening, there were fireworks and a fancy-dress ball. Most of the passengers who had been on a cruise before had come prepared for the latter but the naval personnel had no costumes so had to make do with what they could find. Sheikh Ali Khalifa was outraged to find he was not the only Sheikh in the place. Looking magnificent in silk and velvet, he seemed to believe that the motley assortment of Arabs dressed in tablecloths, dressing gowns, and tea towels was a deliberate insult, and sulked for most of the evening. Mary went as a sailor. She had had little time to prepare her own outfit as she was busy organizing Gully. She dressed him in a pair of pale blue silk pyjamas, and although the legs were a little short, the whole outfit gave him a vaguely eastern look. She shaved his hairy shins and borrowed a pair of eastern slippers from the purser's store of dressing-up things. She made up a gold turban from an evening stole. She stuffed a bra with cotton wool and, because he was so much broader than her, tied the ends together with tape.

"Mary," he said grinning at her, "you've given me some very alluring curves. Have you overdone it?"

"Not at all; you look beautiful!" She made him up carefully, although he refused the lipstick. He was greeted with catcalls and whistles when he went into the bar.

Mary thought it was one of the most fun days that she had ever had. She went to bed and the next day woke to the 20 May. Thanks to crossing the International Date Line, she never got the 19 May back.

Some days later, she was sitting on deck reading when to her surprise the captain approached. He crouched down beside her and took her hand. He looked very serious.

"Goodness, Captain, you look solemn. What's the matter?"

"Mrs Stewart, I've got some terrible news for you, from home."

She felt breathless and her hands chilled. She clutched his arm. "Tell me! Oh God, what is it? Is it my husband? Is it Colin?" She stared at him with a pounding heart and a dry mouth.

"No! No! It's nothing like that. It's not that personal. Well, it is in a way, I suppose. It's your ship; it's HMS *Hood*. She's been sunk."

She stared at him in disbelief. "The *Hood*? HMS *Hood*? The mighty *Hood*? No! It's not possible! She is so fast, so powerful, so strong. It must be a mistake!"

"No mistake, I'm afraid. All ships are vulnerable, Mrs Stewart, even big powerful ones. It happened yesterday, the twenty-fourth. I will tell you more as soon as I know. I wanted to tell you myself. I did not want you to hear it as gossip. I am sure you will be truly distressed by this news."

"Who sunk her, and how many survivors?"

"I don't know the attacker yet; and I don't know about survivors. I will try to find out more. I'm so sorry to bring you this news."

Gully sat quietly beside her all afternoon, just holding her hand. His silence was a comfort. One by one his friends passed by but didn't speak, just smiled and nodded or touched her arm. Even Sheikh Ali, who had remarked in the past that Britain was "finished", had the grace to pass her a small note with

"Sorry" scribbled on it. She thought of men in the lifeboats or clinging desperately to floating debris and wept helplessly. Her own experience came vividly back to life again.

The news, next day, was even worse. There were no survivors. A torpedo from her attacker, the *Bismarck*, had hit the powder magazine and the *Hood* simply exploded. Later Mary learned that there were in fact survivors, three in all, from a ship's complement of over 1,300 men. The *Hood* had been built in the John Brown shipyard where Mary's father had worked. It seemed a personal loss. She could not bring herself to be in the same room as the Germans and left the bar or lounge if she found them there or if they came in. She felt consumed with rage and grief.

27

Arrival in Kobe: American Unease and the Sinking of the Bismarck

*V*ery few passengers went ashore at Kobe and none of the American servicemen. Mary did not know if this was personal choice or if it was orders from "on high". After ten days at sea she was keen to stretch her legs and announced her intention of going, so in the end Gully went with her. If it was an order, he disobeyed it. She was delighted with his company and smiled up at him with real pleasure.

"Why did you change your mind?"

"Why do you think? I shouldn't do this really. There's bad blood between the States and Japan at the moment," he explained. "Well, has been for some time actually. Japan is very militaristic. You know they have invaded parts of China and Manchuria so we've put an embargo on their oil supply. They aren't very happy about that. I think they have other territorial ambitions too! It's all very tense."

"Is it going to develop into something serious?"

"Probably not. The smooth-talking diplomats will sort it out. Usually when there's a lot of sabre rattling it's just that: sabre rattling."

The ship's anchorage was not far from the centre of town, so once ashore they set off on foot. It was a beautiful day. They strolled along the Bund, which ran beside the waterfront, and, avoiding the persistent street hawkers, eventually went into a teahouse, where a smiling girl wearing a kimono and curious wooden sandals called "geta", with stilts on the soles, served them tea and sweet sticky rice cakes. They sat and watched the people passing. The variety of transport fascinated Mary. Rickshaws jostled happily with motorbikes, bicycles, and cars, and there were even carts pulled by oxen. It was a bustling, noisy city. There was a great deal of hooting, shouting, and waving of arms, and what she thought was good-natured abuse.

Mr Hetherington, the second purser, had recommended that Mary save her money for Shanghai, where he said the shops were superior. However, in a busy market off the main thoroughfare she couldn't resist two small Satsuma-ware bowls, lustrous and beautifully coloured. Later they found a shop selling bonsai. They were quite beautiful – tiny trees of every species, shape, and size. One, an exquisite maple, was grown in a whole orange skin. The shopkeeper told her it was forty years old and his father had planted it! Gully wanted to make her a present of it but although tempted, she refused.

"It will probably die on me. I am sure it needs a great deal of care. I can't even keep an aspidistra alive." She laughed, remembering the many plants given to her, which, from neglect or ignorance, had yellowed and withered, before being consigned to the dustbin. She touched the delicate leaves gently and, smiling, refused to bargain for it to the disappointment of the vendor. It was not the real reason for her rejection. Despite their beauty, Mary felt there was something unnatural and even decadent about the tiny trees. The twisted constrained root ball reminded her of the bound feet of Chinese women. The roots permanently struggling to be free, and yet relentlessly confined, must cause suffering. The gnarled trunks and contorted branches she thought told their own tale.

They returned to the ship in the evening, as it was due to sail that night. On board, thirty Japanese tourists had enlarged the complement.

"They do nothing but bow and smile," Gully remarked. "All that deference and affability is very suspect. You never get to look them in the eye." It was the first time Mary had heard him say anything other than easy-going commentary. She was surprised at his irritation.

"That's because they only come up to your shoulder! They are not very tall as a race, are they? I find it very pleasant not to have to crane my neck all the time."

"You never complain about me," was the riposte.

"You're different," she replied shyly.

After the war, when stories of appalling Japanese brutality began to emerge, she found it hard to reconcile the dreadful accounts with the quiet, charming, polite, and cultured companions of her sea voyage.

The same could not be said for the Germans.

27 MAY

Coming into the dining room for dinner two days later, Mary faced a totally unexpected barrage of abuse and invective from them. The couple stood up to address her across the room. He was ashen with fury and his wife in tears. As he was speaking in German, Mary had not the faintest idea what he was saying or what this rage and aggression meant. She stared up into his contorted face, spittle flying from his lips. He seemed to represent all that was loathsome about Germany at that time. Her friends rushed to protect her, forming a human shield.

Above the hubbub, she heard Gully shouting, "It's the *Bismarck*. Your navy have sunk her. Good for them! That ship will do you no more harm." She was trembling as he led her away, but felt it to be a personal reassurance. Outside the purser's office, Mary read the report. The language was dramatic but succinct:

"Hungry for vengeance, the British Navy went in pursuit of its most threatening enemy."

She was torn between exhilaration and horror. She thought of the doomed vessel, shelled mercilessly from sea and air, like a wounded animal worried by dogs. She learned later that damage to the ship's rudder meant the vessel could only turn helplessly in circles. Part of her rejoiced that it would inflict no more damage. But once again she thought of the men in the water, drowning in oil, gagging, choking, and gasping for air. After her own experience and remembering the compassion in Captain Starr's voice as he looked down on the *Graf Spee*, she was so divided by relief at the end of that terrifying menace and pity for the crew, she hardly knew herself.

The captain came to apologize. "I have spoken to Herr Danker and his wife and explained that this is a neutral zone and I will not tolerate such behaviour. I pointed out that you said nothing to him about the sinking of the *Hood*. I expect the same civility from him. However, I believe he has some excuse, as Frau Danker had a seventeen-year-old nephew on board the *Bismarck*."

"Were there any survivors?"

"I believe there were a hundred or so. Not many from a crew of over 2,000."

"That's more than the *Hood*." She hesitated. "Will you come with me to talk to Herr and Frau Danker?"

In the lounge, she found the couple sitting quietly. They stood, she thought apprehensively, as she approached.

"Mrs Stewart has something to say to you, and I hope you will listen to her calmly and civilly." The captain was clearly ready to take a firm line.

Mary took a deep breath. *I hope to God I can get through this*, she thought.

"Frau Danker, I am very sorry about your nephew and sincerely hope he has survived. Our countries are at war, which in itself is tragic, but we are on neutral territory here, and although I don't think we can be friends, I would like to think we can be polite to each other. We have both had terrible news from home. In theory we may be enemies, but surely we can feel mutual compassion for our losses. I hope you believe I am sincere."

"Well done, Mrs Stewart. Bravely said," the captain commented. He looked at the Dankers, clearly expecting a response. There was a long silence then Herr Danker came forward very punctiliously, took her hand and shook it. "I apologize for my outburst; it was very incorrect. Yes, of course we can be civil. You and I personally are not combatants, and this is America. Let us hope for better times when our countries are united again as they were in the past."

She felt a great sense of relief and although their interaction was minimal, from then on they did at least acknowledge each other with a nod and occasionally a quiet "good morning".

Stolen Chopsticks and Love Games

There was a three-day stay in Shanghai and the captain sent round an advice sheet as helpful as it was ambiguous. It was more in what he didn't say than what he did. Delightful as the surrounding countryside was, he seriously advised not straying further afield than the city itself, the Bund, Nanking Road, and the suburbs of the French and the International Concession, mainly Bubbling Well Road. This was where the affluent European expats had settled since the eighteenth century. He made no reference to the Japanese presence in China but neither did he exclude the Japanese passengers from this advice; it was all perfectly anodyne. The Europeans and the Americans listened intently; the Japanese smiled and nodded like adults indulging a child. It filled Mary with unease.

Nothing had prepared her for Shanghai – not its affluence, its beauty, nor its self-confidence. She knew it was called the "Pearl of the Orient" and reckoned the "Paris of the East", and now she knew why. The city seemed to shimmer, silver light dancing off the river and sparkling from white facades. The Bund's extraordinarily diverse architecture – classical, art deco, rococo – was rooted in its colonial past, yet all seemed so actual, so business-like, so modern, so international. She saw no one, including the Chinese, who was not dressed in formal European office wear, men and women alike. The only exception – and they seemed a breed apart – were the rickshaw-pullers squatting patiently by the pavement. In the centre of the road, drawn up, was a line of large limousines, the Chinese chauffeurs leaning against them and chatting to each other or polishing a bonnet or wing if they saw their owners returning to their cars.

Mary and Gully found a café and sat outside drinking strong, creamy coffee, people-watching, and looking at the boat-lined waterfront. Further out, junks sailed majestically by, and smaller vessels dodged between. A smell of camphor wood floated on the air and Mary felt heady with it and smiled at Gully. Later they wandered inland towards Nanking Road, the main shopping area, as recommended by the purser. The shops, according to Mary, were "fabulous". Even in LA or San Francisco she had not seen such wonderful, opulent merchandise; London's Oxford Street looked positively provincial in comparison.

Exquisite clothes filled the windows of the larger stores; the style, quality, and elegance were breathtaking. Smaller intimate boutiques boasted silk lingerie. There were shops selling bed and table linen, wonderfully hand-embroidered, and others full of ornaments, intricate and beautifully carved. There was chinaware and porcelain, while other shops sold fine art, furniture, and paintings. She pressed her face against a window selling sumptuous furs: sable, mink, Russian wolf, and snow leopard.

"Mary," Gully said, laughing and pulling her away, "you live in a moderate climate; you have no use for sable, mink, Russian wolf or snow leopard." Reluctantly, she could only agree. Later they passed a shop selling the most gorgeous jade and ivory.

"Careful," he warned her again. "Some of the so-called jade is soap stone."

"Well, I don't care about that," she laughed. "It's so pretty, it doesn't matter, but I don't want to pay for jade if it isn't. Do you know the difference?"

He confessed he didn't, so she bought a small group of leaping dolphins made either of jade or soap stone for her mother. Because of the price, she suspected the latter. She also bought a pretty set of Chinese chequers in the green stone, whatever it was, for Colin, and incongruously a pipe.

"Is your husband a pipe smoker?" asked Gully, grinning cheekily at her as if he knew the answer.

"I don't know," she answered, almost crossly. It occurred to her that she actually knew very little about her husband's habits. "He smokes cigarettes."

"Don't you think you might do better to buy him a cigarette box?" he suggested gently. She went straight back into the shop and exchanged the pipe for a pretty box with brass corners.

One of the things she noticed, almost straightaway, was the stylishness of the women she passed in the street. Both Chinese and Europeans, it seemed to her, carried an air of unconscious sophistication. In particular, the Europeans moved around on slender legs shod in calfskin shoes as if they owned the very earth they trod on.

"They look so at home, not a bit like expatriates," Mary remarked.

This self-assurance, she thought, was not just colonial: it was imperialist, yet she saw no sullen resentment of it from the Chinese. Everywhere there were willing smiling faces and politeness.

Occasionally there was a jarring note. She saw two elderly Chinese ladies being handed down from their rickshaws and realized immediately, by their short tottering gait and tiny shoes, that they had bound feet. She shuddered, thinking of their maimed, confined toes and remembered the bonsai trees with their tortured roots.

Later they met a little collection of children coming out of an imposing Catholic church. They were all in school uniform – grey blazers – the little girls wearing straw hats. Were it not for the cohort of *amahs* following them and escorting them across the road to where their chauffeured cars awaited them, it could easily have been Guildford or Esher. She turned to Gully in astonishment, though as he had never visited England she did not really expect him to see the similarity. He tried to understand the reference.

"Well," he said, "I expect many of the Brits have lived here for a long time; some maybe having been born here. This is their hometown; that's why they look so at ease. They've got schools, churches, clubs, restaurants, all of which hark back to England. But I think you would find there is almost no social interaction between the indigenous inhabitants and the colonials."

She felt puzzled and momentarily saddened by it. Later she saw how true this was.

At the end of the morning, on Gully's recommendation, she went to a tailor and ordered a lightweight suit in raw silk and two linen dresses to be made for her. She couldn't believe that things could be ready so quickly. Why did it take a week in England to have a hem taken up? She was asked politely to go for a first fitting later in the day, a second next afternoon, and the final in the evening. They promised to deliver the finished garments to the ship.

After lunch, they came upon a crowd of young Chinese queuing in front of a large building called The Wing On and curiosity drew them. It was an indoor roller-skating rink. The arena was floodlit and air-conditioned and rows of spectator seats surrounded it.

"Oh, do let's," said Mary laughing. "It's years since I've been roller-skating." They were the only Europeans in the place and the object of intense interest and curiosity. The manager came to welcome them personally. He spoke good English.

Oh yes, he assured them: roller-skating was the new passion. He was quite overwhelmed when Mary shook his hand.

"You've given him face," Gully assured her. He smiled at her puzzled face.

"What's that?"

"Prestige, dignity – it's very important to the Chinese." He laughed, "He'll probably ask you to marry him." On that ludicrous note, they put on their boots and set off skating. They spent a happy hour at that pleasant juvenile activity. Many there were attracted by the novelty of non-Chinese participants willing to skate with them, so they were often surrounded by a little group of people who sometimes skated backwards to peer into their faces, and seemed eager to interact with them, as if they were celebrities. Mary was torn between charm and embarrassment. Gully stayed close, fending off the rather too keen with a pleasant smile but a firm hand. They paused at the refreshment bar for lemonade and Gully reiterated his comment about the lack of social interaction between the native inhabitants and the expats. "No white faces here," he said. "No wonder they are excited about us." They were shown out when they left, with enthusiastic invitations to come back.

"No cost," the manager assured them. "No cost for such honoured clients."

They took a taxi out to Bubbling Well Road, still within the International Concession, to admire the homes of the "wealthy foreigners", and strolled arm in arm along a long tree-lined alley. They were both astounded. "This is money," Gully said seriously.

The Bund with its colonial references was understandable, but this was faux-Home Counties. Every style was there. They looked through the gates at the Stockbroker Tudor, Neo-Georgian, Gothic revival, Victorian, and Arts and Crafts dwellings, with their immaculately shaven, emerald green lawns. It could have been the county of Surrey, were it not for the occasional sight of white-coated Chinese servants moving calmly but purposefully around. The flowering shrubs and herbaceous borders seemed somehow, despite their beauty, incongruous, as odd as the beamed gables, the herringbone brickwork, and the classical pillars of the domestic dwellings themselves.

They returned to the city for Mary's first fitting then went to find somewhere for dinner.

"Chinese, Italian, Spanish, French, or English?" Gully asked, grinning. He chose Chinese and they found a small intimate restaurant. In a private room, they ate dim sum and duck with plum sauce and chicken liver with walnuts and many other dishes that later she could not remember. They drank rice wine; when they left the place, she felt six inches above the ground.

"I stole the chopsticks as a memento," he said, producing them from his sleeve like a conjurer. "But don't worry, I left a big enough tip to cover them."

"Perhaps we should get back to the ship," Mary said, hesitantly.

"Sweet girl," he replied, taking her hand and kissing the palm.

"Sweet boy," she answered, smiling up at him.

They found a tiny hotel run by a Polish woman who smiled benignly and showed them into a delicious room hung with spangled gauze curtains and a bed covered, to Mary's bemused glance, with multi-coloured silk pillows like jewels. The proprietor arrived almost immediately with a carafe of cold wine and a plate of delicious Turkish delight.

"For lovers," she said unambiguously with a charming smile, and then she drew the curtains and left them alone. They spent a night of tenderness and gentle passionate pleasure. Lying beside him in the morning, she watched his sleeping face. He looked very young. She smiled to herself, suddenly realizing that she didn't even know his age. What had happened between them was the special intimacy of two people coming together in a particular moment in time. She felt neither guilt nor shame; only happiness. She knew she should be troubled or dismayed at the very least, but there didn't seem any space for it. It was all the sweeter for being so fleeting and so transitory. It had none of the harrowing emotion of her time with Michael. She was not going to face the pain of shattered dreams or plans, because with Gully there were no dreams or plans. Sometimes she thought she was in free fall, like Alice down the rabbit hole, where all normal rules were suspended.

Waiting for him to wake up, she thought about her status as a married woman. She felt curiously detached from it and despite the memory of a deep affection for her husband, he was beginning to seem a shadowy figure from a different time and a different world. She wondered if all war wives separated from their husbands felt like her. She had had almost no contact with him since his departure for West Africa. Before she had left England, there had been three or four letters, one asking for money, that she had replied to crossly, and then a long silence. Maybe he was angry with her. She wondered what he was making of her interminable travel. He must have had Dr Maxwell's cable, and he could have replied via the firm in Dagenham.

After breakfast they left their silken oasis and Mary went to the tailor for her second fitting. The clothes, beautifully made, needed minimal adjustment. Gully waited for her, sitting on a bench a short walk away, and then rejoined her. Afterwards they passed an easy, delightful morning wandering along the Bund. They didn't speak much but exchanged soft, smiling glances.

Gully announced he had business at the American Consulate and left her on her own for about an hour. She sat in a small park with the world revolving quietly around her, in a bubble of contentment. Unexpectedly she saw the Dankers walking past with a Japanese couple. The latter smiled and waved and she waved back. The Dankers nodded to her with stern faces. She wondered what these two couples could possibly have in common.

After a while she wandered off and found an ice-cream parlour where she was tempted in. She bought a tub flavoured with ginger and honey and, going back to the park, ate it feeling like a little girl. It was delicious. She thought it much better than the ship's ice cream.

She watched a pale and elegant European woman stroll past with two spaniels on a leash. A Chinese servant carrying her coat walked deferentially behind her. A "coolie" rushed forward and held up the traffic to allow her to pass and Mary thought how incongruous it was. The woman didn't even acknowledge him, and the servant dived between the cars to rejoin her mistress.

"You look guilty, like a kid at the cookie jar," said Gully, looking at the ice-cream carton.

"I don't know why I feel embarrassed. There's nothing wrong with eating ice cream. I thought I might have finished it before you returned."

In the afternoon, to escape the heat and humidity, they went into a theatre and sat entranced, if bemused, by a long Chinese opera as dramatic, colourful, and bloodthirsty as it was incomprehensible. There was a programme but as it was in Chinese they had no idea of the plot. Once again, they were the only non-Chinese in the place. They came out giggling to discover that it was already evening. At the tailor, the outfits she had ordered were ready. Gully offered to carry the parcels but the tailor look shocked and said firmly they would be delivered to her cabin. Clearly, he was scandalized at the idea of a European woman carrying her own packages.

They dined at a fish restaurant on the waterfront and found themselves surrounded by most of the ship's crew and many of the passengers.

"It's obviously popular and well known," said Mary wryly, but she didn't mind that she was seen with Gully. "Do you think they know?" she asked him.

He laughed aloud, taking her hand across the table. "Sweet girl," he said, "of course they know. It's written all over your face and over mine too."

Back on board she was pleased yet relieved to find all her packages lying on her bed.

Going to bed that night she found the cabin opposite was now occupied. Her new neighbour was a nun. Mary had only ever seen one at a distance. There was no convent in Dunoon. In her youth in Glasgow she had occasionally seen them and had always felt uneasy at their exotic medieval appearance. This one, Mary thought, looked like a magpie, with her white dress and black veil. Her age was indeterminate but she had a round dimpled face and a sweet smile. She was Chinese but spoke beautiful English. She was friendly and pleasant and, over the next few days, Mary came to know her and to like her very much indeed. Her name was Sister Maria Angelina and she was going to Bombay to rejoin her convent there.

She had been to visit her sick mother in Shanghai she told Mary, and had been away from her convent for three months. "I'm just longing to get back," she said. She didn't come into the bar but sat in the lounge in the evening, happy to play Chinese chequers, at which she was an expert, or just talk. First thing in the morning and just before going to bed she paced up and down the deck reading from a small black book.

"It's my office book, my prayer book. Each day we have seven periods of prayer called the hours and I enjoy the first and last one of the day outside." She always had a glass of wine with lunch and dinner, which surprised Mary. "I thought missionaries didn't drink."

"I'm not a Methodist or a Presbyterian. I am a Roman Catholic and there is nothing in our Holy Rule about not drinking wine. Think of all the wine that Jesus produced at the marriage in Cana."

Mary was very struck by this, and wondered what her Presbyterian minister in Dunoon would have made of it.

Interlude

My mother's persistent reluctance to join any family get-together, other than Christmas when I insisted she join us for dinner, was puzzling for me. All her descriptions of her young life revealed a vibrant, gregarious person who actually relished company and sought it out. When had she become so reclusive? My efforts to get her out once a week to a local social club lunch had been fruitless.

"The food was dreadful," she told me, "and I've nothing to say to people like that. I have nothing in common with them." I could have considered this overt snobbishness but it was more an intellectual isolationism. She had no time either for my sweet mother-in-law Eveline. Although she was fond of her and thought her charming, she also found her "badly educated and ill read".

She dismissed my reproof. It was my brother who pointed out that service life in the fifties was not conducive to the maintenance of long-term friendships. People met, were friendly for a time, and then got posted to the other end of the world. I accepted this but on further reflection remembered her difficulty with some aspects of army social life. Although she loved the balls, dinners, and sports events, she loathed others. She would attend a cocktail party out of duty and not for pleasure. I never knew her accompany my father to the mess for a drink on a Sunday morning. With one or two rare exceptions, she despised his fellow officers. "They have absolutely no conversation," she told me contemptuously, "and talk shop, military shop, the whole time. Their wives are no better, just ciphers."

Even in civilian life, after my father left the services, she made no permanent friends. She had many acquaintances, people with whom she exchanged the time of day, may even have invited to tea or coffee, but no intimates, and nothing durable. Village life seemed to isolate her further.

Perhaps being a Catholic was unhelpful. In a small country community, much of the social life revolves around the parish church, and few villages have both Anglican and Roman Catholic ones. In the fifties and sixties, the latter had a rigid moratorium on any participation with the Anglican Communion. Catholics were forbidden to attend any non-Catholic services, including marriages and christenings, and even social events were discouraged.

I recognized, also, that both my parents were very protective of their acquired status and avoided anything that would link them to those they would have considered social inferiors. Both of them came from a working-class background, which made them particularly sensitive to that.

Later in life, in Brighton, my mother did establish some tenuous friendships: one couple came to visit her when she moved to Portsmouth, and she exchanged Christmas cards with others. The estate agent for whom she worked in Brighton valued her and was considered by her to be a friend, yet she was never invited to his home and had no social interaction with him and his family. She was friendly with Dorothy, my brother's mother-in-law; they went on holiday together once or twice. She even took some poor young permanently relapsing alcoholic under her wing and brought her home for supper from time to time. Clearly, she didn't feel her social status was under any threat from her.

She could be particularly unpleasant occasionally. Once I persuaded her downstairs to meet friends invited to a dinner party and asked afterwards, still in the glow of a successful evening, what she thought of one guest. I commented, "Beatrice is so lovely, isn't she?" My mother's response dumbfounded me. "Oh, you can meet women like her any day of the week." Was this jealousy, resentment or fear? Perhaps she recognized that Beatrice, too, had climbed the greasy pole.

These were all things that I thought about for hours after our evening conversations. When had she changed, and why and what, if anything, could I – should I – do about it?

29

Hong Kong:
"Land of the Fragrant Streams"

A tap on her door woke her.

"Mary, it's Sister Maria Angelina. You really ought to get up and see this!"

Still in her pyjamas and dressing gown, Mary hurried out into the passage and up the stairs to the deck. *The last time I did this*, she thought crossly, *I ended up in a lifeboat. I hope this is not a repeat performance.*

Fortunately, in this instance, there were no alarm bells or sirens.

The rails were crowded with passengers, some dressed but others, like herself, still in their nightwear. It created a very informal atmosphere. Maria Angelina waved to her. "Over here. I've saved you a place." As Mary squeezed in beside her and pressed against the rail, she said, "Just by chance I saw a notice put up by the purser last night – 'Get up for a dawn arrival in Hong Kong.' You'd gone to bed and I didn't want to disturb you."

Mary felt herself blush. Gully had come to her cabin for an hour or so after dinner. She could only be grateful for the nun's naïvety or her discretion. Mary suspected the latter.

Hong Kong harbour at 5:30 a.m. on 1 June was a kaleidoscope of colour. As the sun rose, the hills of the Peak on the island, and the more distant ones on the Kowloon side, were pale purple, tinged with pink. Groups of elegant houses close to the waterfront were silhouetted against the delicate pastel shade of the hillside. The residential district of the Peak looked enchanting; white houses tucked away in green groves. A tall elegant building in a vaguely art-deco style, very prominent among the lower buildings of the business centre, was the new Hong Kong and Shanghai Bank.

"It's air-conditioned!" Sister Maria Angelina said. "Imagine working in such a hot place and yet all around you cool air."

"I bet they have colds all the time," said Mary prosaically. "Very injurious to the health, a continual change of temperature." She wasn't sure if this was true, but it was the sort of thing her mother said and Mary was prepared to give it the benefit of the doubt. She hadn't noticed any bad effect from the air-conditioned roller-skating rink in Shanghai but that had only been for an hour or so.

Unexpectedly Gully arrived with a pair of binoculars and for the next half an hour they trained the glasses on the lovely island, commenting and exclaiming as they discovered other interesting views. The harbour was full of junks – those strange stately vessels with their brown fan-like sails.

At 7:30 a.m. stewards brought round tea, coffee, and hot chocolate. The atmosphere was positively festive.

With the ship at anchor in the harbour, little boats full of small boys diving for pennies surrounded them. Small lithe Chinese lads, some looking barely five years of age, shouted, grinned, and waved, their skinny bodies glistening with water.

"Hello Sister nun; hello lady; hello sailor man! You got dimes? You got dollars?"

Mary was horrified at the depth they might have to dive for such small return and began to throw dollars over the side, until Sister Maria Angelina pulled at her arms, laughing.

"They do this all day," said Gully. "They probably make a good living at it."

This could be true, thought Mary. Many years later, the memory of those bright, brown, grinning lads re-surfaced when beggar children in Rome accosted her. She watched uneasily as they trooped into the bar where she was having coffee, handing their gains over to a mean-faced Italian seated in a corner reading a newspaper. In retrospect, she wondered how much the mud larks had taken home.

Other small boats, which Sister Maria Angelina called "sampans", arrived, offering anything from fruit to lengths of brocade and ornaments. Shouted negotiations were carried on and when a price was agreed, a basket was lowered so the goods could be hauled up and inspected and either purchased or returned. Mary was amazed how long people were prepared to bargain and haggle over such small sums and for such shoddy goods.

"It's all part of the fun," said Gully, grinning. "Are you sure you don't want a fat brass Buddha or a dragon? I would be pleased to haggle for you."

He put his arm round her and she, indifferent to who noticed, leaned back against him. Sister Maria Angelina glanced at them, looked away and smiled. Her face was kind.

Over breakfast they discussed how different Hong Kong was from Shanghai. They agreed that comparisons were difficult. "Hong Kong is a Crown colony," remarked Mr Hetherington, the second purser, "run by the British for the British. I can't say whether that's good or bad but it makes for stability. Shanghai is an international city, even with the Japanese snapping at its heels. It's like comparing a delicate watercolour to an oil painting; both wonderful but quite different in style and execution."

The ship was due to sail at 10 p.m. that same day, so immediately after breakfast Mary and Gully took a boat to the island and set off for the Peak funicular railway. The day was bright and warm. The little train rattled precipitously upwards. It took about fifteen minutes to reach the top. Mary noticed that the Chinese using it were, in the main, servants. Gully said he had heard that only Europeans were allowed to live on the Peak. This ruling had been revoked, Mary learned, in the thirties, but the train was still reserved for Europeans during the business rush hour and the two front benches were retained permanently for the governor just in case he should arrive unexpectedly.

"We'll sit here anyway," said Mary firmly. "It's got the best view and if he comes I'll move." They were left undisturbed; there was no sudden appearance of the governor, rather to Mary's secret disappointment – and to Gully's relief.

"It's all very well for you, you're just a girl, a sweet, sassy civilian, but I'm an American naval officer. If there are rules, they have to be obeyed."

The view from the top was spectacularly beautiful. The slopes of the Peak flowed, a sea of green, down to the city below. The harbour was full of ships of every shape and size: naval vessels, junks, and sampans, motor boats zig-zagging between them. Gully pointed out the green and white Star Ferries moving in a straight line between the island and the mainland.

"If we've got time we'll go across. I'm told it's more authentically Chinese over there," Gully said.

Across the harbour the peninsular stretched away, Kowloon town: colourful, busy and animated, the residential area behind it reaching out until habitation gradually gave way to the rich vegetation of the countryside, abruptly ending at a range of grey mountains, one shaped like a lion's head. Beyond the mountains, the New Territories with its hundreds of rice paddies stretched out towards the immensity of China.

They decided to walk down from the Peak. It was a metalled road but shaded by trees and thick undergrowth. They were quite alone. A solitary car passed them going downhill. They were too far above the city for traffic noise. It was, Mary said, positively bucolic. Once or twice, the vista opened and they passed still, silent, brown ponds covered with creamy water lilies, the surface broken by turtles swimming indolently around, their craggy wrinkled heads poking above the water, others basking on flat rocks. The air was filled with the harsh croaking of frogs, and huge multi-coloured butterflies flitted among the undergrowth. Unfamiliar birds wheeled overhead, emitting occasional raucous cries. The sun cast mottled shadows from the vegetation, dappling the road and their faces. They were both enchanted, and exclaimed and laughed with shared pleasure.

When they began to reach houses they took rickshaws down into the city. Mary always felt uncomfortable in rickshaws. From her seat under the shade of the hood, she stared down at the wiry muscled back of the coolie pulling it. Sweat ran in rivers between his bony shoulder blades. The slap-slap of his sandaled feet on the tarmac reinforced the impression that she was being transported somewhere by a human beast of burden. She felt shame as well as embarrassment. She always paid over the odds, which she recognized was to assuage her guilt.

They found a pleasant restaurant for lunch, a little back from the waterfront, in the Wang Hing Building. They sat with their knees touching under the table and smiled at each other. Fifteen years later, Mary was to work there on the third floor as personal secretary to Mr Stewart of Stewart & Co., "Solicitors to the Crown".

Gully returned to the ship to attend a naval meeting, having decided he couldn't afford the time to cross the harbour. Mary, feeling brave and independent, took the Star Ferry across to the Kowloon side. In the tall spacious lobby of the Peninsula Hotel, she ordered tea and sat thinking about life and love and adventures on the high seas. Above her head fans rotated gently. Surprisingly, there was no air-conditioning in the hotel. Mary always felt that the fans were mainly ineffective and did nothing except cut the hot air into chunks, but she accepted, grudgingly, that when the temperature really rose they were better than nothing.

She sipped her tea and sank down into the plump armchair. She was suddenly pleased to be on her own and have time to pause. She felt that life was rushing past at such a speed; she barely had time to assimilate one set of circumstances before being precipitated into the next. In that large, elegant, cool and comfortable place, the little music quartet on the balcony played pleasantly. She listened to the murmuring rise and fall of conversation, broken sometimes with laughter or a raised voice, the chink of teacups, the occasional rasp of a match being struck. Someone nearby was smoking a pungent cigarette – Gauloises or maybe Turkish tobacco. Soft-shoed waiters in pristine white mandarin-collared tunics moved quietly among the guests. She looked at the fronds of the palms and lilies stacked in tall vases; they moved gently, stirred by the fans. She slipped into a quiet and relaxed half-sleep.

Shadowy figures peopled her rest, all of them pleasant: Dr Maxwell smiling at her across his desk; Colin painting her sitting room; Ted Boddle arguing about crossword clues; dear Mrs Harrison knitting; Miss Phelps with her thin sunburned legs and gentle smile; the Gué family; Charlie Chaplin and his handsome craggy-faced young male companion who was "going to make it big"; "Tweedledum and Tweedledee"; the cooing and twittering Chinese telephonists in San Francisco. The outside world faded.

The anxious waiter brought her back to reality. "Madam, are you well? Can we bring you more tea?" She was aware that her cheeks were wet; with tears or sweat, she didn't know which. Her daydreaming had been happy. Not once had memories of the lifeboat, nor of the deaths she had seen, intruded, but she felt dazed and wondered if she had a little heat stroke from her walk down from the Peak; she had worn no hat. She sat up, groped for her bag, and found her cigarettes. She took several deep breaths and smiled at the anxious face of the waiter.

"Thank you," she said firmly. "I am quite well, just a little tired. A glass of water and more tea would be delicious."

Back on board she found the ship quiet, the decks and bar deserted; many passengers were still ashore. There was no sign of Gully, but in the lounge she found Sister Maria Angelina with three or four other nuns, obviously come to visit, who made pleasant and polite conversation. Eventually she excused herself and found her cabin. She lay down and although she didn't sleep, she rested. Struggling to understand her mood, she decided she was suffering not from heat but from travel fatigue. She had been away from England for two-and-a-half months, and still had seven weeks before she reached her destination. She had lost count of how many hotels she had stayed in, how many times she had packed and unpacked her suitcase, how many times she had said goodbye. Who was it, she thought, who had been destined to travel for ever? Was it some creature from Greek mythology or from the Bible? Was it the "Wandering Jew", condemned to walk the earth until the Second Coming? Was it poor Ulysses, taking ten years to get home to faithful, long-suffering Penelope? She felt very sympathetic towards them all. India was beginning to feel unimaginably far off – as far off in fact as Dunoon. Was she destined to sail round the world and actually never arrive? It was beginning to feel like it.

I'm tired, she thought, *tired of the exotic. I want to reach a safe harbour, familiar faces, set up my own place and stay quietly for at least a year.*

Gully found her in the bar before dinner. He seemed to know without her saying that she was troubled, and she was very relieved that he neither interrogated her nor tried to jolly her along. She thought how calm and reassuring he was, how instinctively sympathetic, and how much she could have been happy with him.

30

Jai Alai and a Medical Emergency

The ship spent four days in Manila, the longest stop of the voyage. The weather was oppressively hot and humid – the air stagnant, the sky leaden and the light an odd murky green – so it was a relief when at the end of the first afternoon there was a thunderstorm and a torrential downpour. Rain flooded the street, sweeping debris, paper, and sinister unidentifiable jetsam before it. Water bounced knee-high off the pavement. Mary and Gully, rushing to take cover, found refuge in a church, where Mary was overwhelmed by the plethora of statues, votive lamps, and candles – all brightly coloured and gilded. She had been in a Catholic church before with Michael, and had noted the iconography, if she were honest, with some distaste, but this was unbelievably garish. The altar was crowded with silver candelabra, on either side statues proliferated, some even clothed in silk and spangled dresses, their cerulean veils or headdresses trimmed with velvet ribbon and lace. She found it difficult to think that these were cult objects worthy of veneration. She looked around dazed; the scent of incense was powerful. A simpering plaster statue stood near the door, her arms full of roses.

"I've seen this before," Gully whispered, "in Mexico. It's just a tradition, a style; doesn't mean they aren't good Christians. Look at your guardsmen, all dressed up in scarlet and gold, plumed hats and brass bucklers or whatever they are. It's the outward sign – it doesn't mean they aren't good soldiers."

"I suppose not," said Mary hesitantly. "It's just so very different from the kirk at home."

There were two or three elderly ladies, dressed all in black, seated in a side chapel. Rosary beads slipped between their fingers as they whispered to each other, their heads nodding, their faces illuminated by the flickering candles. Mary thought irresistibly of Macbeth's three witches, then she realized they were praying and was torn between remorse and amusement. Occasionally one or the other would draw her lacy headscarf further over her forehead, the fingernails of her old wrinkled hands incongruously painted scarlet. Gully suggested in Mary's ear that they, too, had taken shelter from the rain. Eventually one rose to light a candle and the others joined her. They paused before the altar and genuflected before turning to leave. All three of them gave a formal bow of the head, dignified and gracious. Mary wished she hadn't compared them to the three witches.

Outside the pavements steamed but the air was fresher. The streets were busy; as in Kobe the cars jostled for space with horse-drawn carts. Some were more carriages than carts, prettily painted and hung with ribbons. The occupants were mainly Filipino women, black-haired and olive-skinned. They had a lustrous opulent beauty.

The main thoroughfares were elegant, the buildings acknowledging a Spanish influence. There were more modern buildings too, and art deco was clearly a favourite style. Gully surprised her, saying he had tickets for a match that afternoon that he thought she might enjoy. The purser had offered them. After consulting the address on the ticket, they made their way to the Jai Alai Palace, a new purpose-built stadium named after the very popular national game, jai alai.

"Whatever made you think I'd like this?" she asked teasingly. She didn't really care what they did; it was enough they were together.

"It's fast and furious by all accounts and very skilled, and they don't play it in Scotland so it's a whole new experience. And it's air-conditioned. Come on, Mary, live a little!"

"How you can say that to *me*, I don't know." However, she shrugged, laughed, took his arm and went in. Spectators sat in tiered ranks overlooking a large court. The game was dazzlingly spectacular, similar to squash but faster and fiercer. The ball, thrown from a hand-held curved basket, bounced off the walls and floors. The spectator participation was raucous. Mary and Gully joined in the cheering at particularly skilful manoeuvres and gasped at near misses or amazing recoveries. They watched two or three matches and then left. Gully said he felt exhausted by the energy expended on the court. However, in the ticket office, they discovered there was an elegant café and restaurant on an upper level and they could have a beer and still see the game. High above the court, it was a tamer participation but interesting to see the activity from a different angle. From that vantage point, the players were foreshortened. Mary remembered with nostalgia the many evenings in the "gods" of London theatres, where, with Sheridan and "K", Shayler and Colin, she had watched musicals and revues looking down at the dwarfed performers, whose voices floated upward through the blue fug of a hundred cigarettes.

Among the spectators, Mary caught sight of a European who seemed vaguely familiar but when she leaned forward to get a better look, he had disappeared. "I know who you've seen," said Gully. "I'll tell you later." Despite her insistence, he refused to be drawn.

Wandering the streets, dropping into cafés, shopping, Mary wondered how much American colonization really affected the life of the indigenous population. You could learn to speak English with an American accent, accept a dual currency, American dollars being "dollars gold" and Filipino dollars being "dollars mex". You could begin to enjoy burgers and hotdogs and understand that a drug store wasn't a pharmacy, learn to chew gum and relish a Hershey bar; nevertheless at home, in school, and at work, Filipino girls were reserved, modest, and shy. Their undoubted handsomeness as a race only served to emphasize their self-possessed restraint. Adults, both men and women, were pleasant and gracious; older people grave and composed. There was none of the Anglo-Saxon brashness and loud self-importance that both British and Americans were occasionally and unfortunately so prone to. The Spanish influence was evident not only in the architecture but in the cultural life. Spanish as well as English was spoken everywhere. She felt that the Americanization of the Philippines was a thin veneer, a coating, just about covering but barely concealing a fierce pride in their national identity.

In the evening, they took a taxi to a waterfront restaurant and sat at a table outside, Gully drinking his favourite rum and Coke and Mary a whisky. "Do you know?" he said suddenly. "I joined the navy to get away from my mother." He grinned ruefully. "Is that terrible?" He had almost never spoken about his family, although she knew he was divorced. She wondered what had provoked this unexpected revelation.

"Well, I went south from Scotland to get away from my family. So we've got that in common," she said, smiling at him. He stared out across the water, narrowing his eyes against the sun, now low in the sky.

"How can you claim to love somebody yet constrain them, aim to control and thwart them every step they take? She broke up my marriage. I was too young anyway. Nineteen! Boy, that's a crazy age to wed, but my poor kid of a wife got no say in our relationship. My mother dominated our whole life even down to our bedroom curtains. Caroline stuck it out eighteen months and then she was off. Couldn't blame her, really. So I was a divorcee at twenty-one. I flew the nest after that and I have never been back. I'm a long way from Oregon now."

Mary recognized some of the same struggles she had faced. *Families*, she thought. She felt very close to him.

In silence they watched the sunset: blue then gold and vermillion, clouds like creamy brush strokes, the sea burnished bronze. "I've got no roots; I don't belong anywhere. The navy is my home, my family, my job, my life." He seemed sad and disheartened. Mary took his hand.

"Oh Gully, sweet boy, you'll find someone: a lovely girl who'll adore you. You will adore each other and you will be very happy together, with lots of kids. You will have a fine house with a big garden and a tree with a swing for the children. Oh, and you'll have a dog." She smiled. "Maybe a Scottie or a West Highland terrier to remind you of me!"

He roared with laughter. "Sweet girl! You really are the tops."

A taxi took them back to the ship. Many people had remained ashore so the dining room was half-empty. Mr Hetherington told Mary that Herr Danker and his wife had disembarked and would be returning to San Francisco on another ship. She had become used to the Dankers' grim Teutonic presence but was glad to see the back of them; she saw that several of the missionaries had also gone. Other passengers were expected to embark before the ship's departure from Manila on 8 June.

Sister Maria Angelina joined them in the lounge later in the evening. She had spent the day with nuns at a Franciscan convent and said she half-wished she had become a nun in their congregation. "They are so down to earth, so simple, so in touch with ordinary people. I feel I should have more direct contact with the poor, the destitute, the people who really need help down at street level. A Dominican life is a bit like living in an ivory tower, you know."

"Can't you change?" asked Gully. "In the navy you can apply to transfer to a different branch."

"Yes, I suppose I could. Actually, I certainly can. Oh dear, I am so troubled. I hardly know myself. But this is just a silly impulse." She laughed shakily. "Maybe I shouldn't go ashore any more." She was clearly distressed, and to Mary's consternation wept a little.

Gully came back from the bar, a cognac in his hand. "Sister," he said, "medicinal purposes only. Get this down you. Have a good night's sleep, remember your sisters in India, and look at the situation in the light of day."

"Goodness!" she said, recovering, blowing her nose and laughing, if tearfully. "I haven't ever drunk spirits. Is this medicinal?"

"Definitely!" said Mary and Gully in unison and they sat happily beside her until Mary took Maria Angelina sleepily and smilingly to her cabin.

At breakfast the next morning she reproached them. "I was thirsty all night and woke with such a headache. You might have warned me! Never again."

"I feel a bit ashamed," Mary said later. "We got a nun drunk. Even if we did it with the best of intentions, it must be a particularly heinous offence!"

Later that afternoon she went ashore again, this time with Mr Hetherington. He offered to advise her about buying a typewriter. She had seen one the previous day and was very taken with it. It was a small portable machine, very neat with a grey travelling case, costing $50 gold. She felt instinctively, as she told him, that it reflected a subconscious urge to get back to work.

Mr Hetherington said he would take it back to the ship and she accepted his offer. Gully and two other naval officers were due to join her for lunch at the restaurant where the previous evening they had watched the sunset. She had brought her swimming costume with her and afterwards they all went down to the beach, lay on the sand under grass umbrellas, sunbathed, chatted, and bathed. She swam out to a raft and sat with her legs in the clear warm water, watching Gully, with his long lazy crawl, come to join her. Below her in the limpid water a myriad tiny silver fish played around her feet. Gully hauled himself onto the raft. They sat side by side and watched other swimmers and the children splashing in the shallows. Their sweet light voices rising and falling travelled across the water. She felt immeasurably happy. It was a relaxed afternoon.

On the way back to the esplanade for a few beers, she saw the European that she had espied briefly at the Jai Alai Palace. She hesitated, shading her eyes. He was some distance off. She noted his crumpled linen suit, but his face was hidden by a large battered straw hat pulled well down over his brow.

"I know that man," she said frowning, "but I just can't place him."

Gully grinned at her.

"You know who he is, don't you?" she said accusingly. "Why won't you tell me?"

He just shook his head and laughed.

The taxi dropped the four of them at the dock gates and they strolled, chatting, toward the ship.

"There he is again," said Mary suddenly, pointing. On a bollard, a figure in a crumpled suit was sitting, swaying slightly, a cigar drooping from his fingers, ash falling onto his trouser leg, his hat on the ground. He turned an affable face toward them, rose, staggered slightly, and bowed to Mary.

"Well," he said, "Little Miss Scotland, don't you know I'm a hobo at heart?" His voice was slurred and his eyes bloodshot.

"He's as drunk as a lord," she said aghast. "It's the ship's doctor! I knew I recognized him but couldn't place him. Whatever should we do?"

"It's a serious offence, even if he's not on duty," said one of Gully's friends. "We've got to get him on board and sobered up before anyone sees him." Between them they manhandled him, staggering up the gangway, Mary scouting ahead to warn them if any of the ship's company appeared. He was difficult to manage, being both heavy and completely uncooperative. As soon as they had him on his feet, he began to struggle frantically, pulling against the restraining arms and lashing out with his fists. This was largely ineffectual, his aim being erratic. Now and again he landed a feeble punch and bellowed triumphantly. Then he yelled, throwing his head back, "Help! I'm being kidnapped."

The scene was like something out of a Buster Keaton film, arms and legs and bodies entangled. Mary began to laugh: it was all so absurd.

With their combined efforts, they reached his cabin, forced him inside and sat him down. If anything, he became more belligerent.

"How dare you? Do you know who I am? I shall report you all."

"Yes, we do know who you are: you are the medical officer and you are drunk!" said one of the Americans. "We will get you some coffee, lots of coffee, then you should take a bath and sober up."

The doctor looked at the four of them standing in a semi-circle around him. He wore the aggrieved faux-dignified expression of the seriously inebriated claiming to be sober. "I'm not ready to come aboard! I want to go into town." Then with a final effort, he bellowed, "Dolores is expecting me! I am perfectly sober!"

"Shut up!" hissed Gully. "Keep your voice down. Do you want everybody in here? Dolores can wait – you can see her tomorrow. Today you are drunk and if you are seen like this, your job is finished."

There was a pregnant silence in the cabin. The doctor bowed his head and sat silently for about thirty seconds, as if considering the situation. Mary bent down to look up into his face, thinking he might have fallen asleep. Then, without warning, he fell sideways off his chair, having passed out.

"We can't just leave him like that," whispered Mary. She found she was hiccoughing with stress and excitement.

"Oh yes we can," replied Gully. "I'll check up in an hour or two, and we'll get Sister Maria Angelina to pray that nobody needs serious medical help for a few hours. If need be, we'll get the ship's nurse to deal with trivial things."

The doctor made no further appearance that night. Gully had found him on his bed when he looked in after dinner, turned him on his side, covered him with a blanket and left him. One of the stewards, who had gone in to the doctor to take him his whisky nightcap at 10:30 p.m. – unnecessarily as it turned out – told Gully such bingeing was common among medical officers.

"Not that I have anything to say about that. He's a perfect gentleman as far as I'm concerned. I'm just saying that I've seen it all before. And not just the doctor!" he added darkly.

"They've been too long at sea," Gully said, referring to this particular tendency. "It takes them that way sometimes."

The following afternoon Mary reported to the ship's surgery for her booster vaccination against typhoid and paratyphoid A and B. This was mandatory for those visiting or living in the tropics and she needed to be protected because of her future prolonged stay in India. She was apprehensive about seeing the doctor in the light of the previous day's events and hoped it would be the nurse. However, it was the man himself. He was as usual pleasant and civil. He was bright-eyed, and if his breath smelled heavily of mint, Mary could only be relieved. He looked her in the face and asked her cheerfully how she liked Manila. She said very much indeed and told him about the Jai Alai game she had watched. She looked carefully at him to judge his reaction. "I went too," he said. "What an extraordinary event!" Then he signed her TAB certificate and handed it to her. "Thank you, Mrs Stewart."

He opened the door for her and as she passed through, he took her hand and repeated, "Thank you, Mrs Stewart." She was uncertain as to the reason for his gratitude.

31

Raffles and a Not-So-Sweet Parting

*M*ary felt there was something deeply unpleasant about Singapore but she couldn't immediately identify the reason for her antipathy. It compared, she thought, very unfavourably with Hong Kong. It was busier and more frenetic. She knew it had a huge naval dockyard and was a significant local employer, with a vast civil service, staffed to a considerable degree by Indians.

However, in terms of comfort the climate was against it. It was less than 100 miles from the equator and barely fifty feet above sea level, so although the heat might have been tolerable, its humidity was seriously unpleasant. Sister Maria Angelina told her it rained every day at 4 p.m. She didn't know if this was true but the air was heavy with moisture and Mary, who almost never sweated, found it distasteful to have hands perpetually moist. Her skirts and blouses stuck to her legs and back. Any exertion, in fact any movement, resulted in a trickle of perspiration down her back, behind her knees, or between her breasts.

The diversity of the ethnic population certainly differentiated it from Hong Kong. Here was a real melting pot: Chinese, Malaysians, Indians (both Hindus and Sikhs), and every possible combination of mixed races jostled with Europeans. The variety was astonishing. On the streets, apart from Chinese and what she assumed was Malay, she heard French, Italian, and Spanish spoken and, on more than one occasion, German.

The city itself with its elegant colonial buildings had the same overweening self-confidence that had impressed her in Shanghai and Hong Kong. The large, and she thought ugly, Anglican cathedral projected a solid image of Anglo-Saxon virtues. There were pleasant tree-shaded squares, the streets were clean, she saw no beggars, the shops were sumptuous, the rickshaws weaved between cars and buses with the same disregard for risk, yet for all that it felt sleazy. "The prostitutes," Mr Hetherington had told her, "are the prettiest and the cleanest in the Far East. But," he added, "crime and drugs are a big problem."

"Decadent, that's the word," she told Gully, fanning herself with the menu card. "It feels decadent."

"Mary! It's three o'clock in the afternoon. You are sitting in the Long Bar of the Raffles Hotel, drinking a Singapore sling, and you'll probably have another when I've finished this beer. There are servants at your beck and call, you only need lift your finger – in fact an eyebrow would probably be good enough. You are in one of the most exotic and famous hotels in the world, and you are here with a man who isn't your husband. That might be described as decadent."

She grinned at him and ignored his comment, then looked around. "I don't see any Chinese or Malays in here. Do you? Do you think they are barred, or do they just choose not to come?"

He looked wryly at her. "I think they were finally allowed in in 1935, or about that time. But if you felt unwelcome even if you were allowed in, would you come? I *have* heard there are Asian guests in the hotel."

They sat chatting and drinking late into the afternoon. As the sun set it became a little cooler but no less humid. They wandered through the lobby of the hotel and along the shady Moorish arcades giving onto courtyards and gardens where fountains played. The small areas of lawn were emerald green. The hotel was magnificent, vast, luxurious, and elegant. "It doesn't have the class of the Peninsula in Kowloon though," Mary said, "and it is a bit like a big white wedding cake, although a very tasteful one."

"Do you want to stay here for the night?" asked Gully. "We can if you like." He gave her his usual shy tender smile. She was piercingly aware of how little remaining time they had together.

"No, thank you. I don't think May & Baker would fund this. Do you? And *we* certainly can't afford it."

She had an appointment for lunch the next day with the head of the May & Baker Singapore office and his wife at the Goodwood Park Country Club, and felt she needed to dress for the occasion. So they went back to the ship and ordered Singapore slings in the bar, which the barman made for them with a wry smile. "I'll be making these till we reach Bombay. Once people get the taste..."

The Goodwood Park Country Club was for Europeans only and here Mary saw what she thought were the colonial ex-patriates at their worst. The May & Baker rep, Mr Rook, and his wife were charming, and lunch was very pleasant, but she cringed at the boorishness of many of the people eating there. The waiters were treated with brusqueness bordering on rudeness and arrogance. Orders were shouted out across the room. "Boy, boy! Another G&T..."; "Where's my beer?"; "I ordered lobster not crab..."; "Take it away..."; "I said well done!... This steak is rare. Don't you understand *well done... well done...* ." Mary didn't think she heard a "please" or "thank you" during the couple of hours she spent there.

It was very different from the Peninsula Hotel, with the civil, calm atmosphere that she had so enjoyed. So it was with relief that she said goodbye, thanked the Rooks, then ordered a taxi and went back to the Raffles Hotel for tea with Gully and several of his fellow officers. Mr Rook had brought letters for her. One from Dr Maxwell, as solicitous as ever, a pleasant brief one from Choppin saying how much he was looking forward to her arrival, but still nothing from Colin. Did he remember he had a wife, she wondered? They had spent so little time together.

Gully took her out to dinner. They found a small restaurant with a balcony hung with lanterns, shielded from the street below by a delicate bamboo screen interwoven with flickering silver lights. In the corner was a sweet-smelling tree with creamy pink blossoms, its branches overhanging the balcony. She thought it could have been an almond or a frangipani. On the floor at her feet it had shed a carpet of petals. When she moved her sandals she felt them drifting over her toes. She thought of butterflies.

On the ceiling small silvery lizards lay in wait for mosquitos and other insects, stalking them patiently then darting with sudden deadly ferocity. Later Mary was quite unable to remember what she had eaten. She had always thought the expression "they looked into each other's eyes" hackneyed, overly sentimental, but later, remembering that evening, she believed that was all they had done.

They returned to the ship about 11 p.m. and he came back to her cabin with her. They had always been more discreet and circumspect on board but tonight they thought it really didn't matter. They lay and talked, laughing at shared memories, at chopsticks stolen, at the rediscovered pleasure of roller-skating. They tried to remember which of the pretentious houses on Bubbling Well Road in Shanghai they had thought the most ludicrous. He teased her about taking the front bench on the funicular in Hong Kong, daring the governor to arrive, and they remembered with pleasure the lovely walk down from the Peak, past the brown lily-covered ponds alive with the turtles. They tried to recreate, in the few short hours still remaining, all the happiness and fun and companionship they had discovered together.

Eventually they fell asleep and when they woke it was daylight and he had to leave. As he opened the cabin door he came face to face with Sister Maria Angelina. He told Mary, after breakfast, he was never more aware of the inscrutability of the Chinese face. "I hadn't the faintest idea what she was thinking. Her face wasn't blank – she looked at me, she even smiled and said good morning – but it beats me what was going through her mind."

Just before noon the entire American naval contingent disembarked. Mary was determined that the last sight Gully had of her would not be a tearful one as Boddle had faced in Montevideo, so she smiled when he put his arms around her, and kissed him back. He put his hand gently to her cheek. "Sweet girl," he said. "Take it easy, take it easy." Then he turned and was gone from her. She watched his slim fair figure go down the gangway, step onto land and then she lost him in the crowd.

Back in her cabin she sat on the bed and wondered why Shakespeare had said parting was such sweet sorrow. She didn't think it was at all sweet! She had no urge now to weep but felt a great sense of loss. She thought, "Why should I cry? It was always going to end like this." There was a tap on the door and when she opened it the nun was outside.

She had an ice-cold Singapore sling on a small tray. She smiled and said sweetly, "I thought you could do with this. Then perhaps you might join me for lunch. What are we going to do without all those merry boys?"

They didn't talk much and when the meal was over, Mary said she would have a swim and write her diary. From the upper deck she watched the nun pacing up and down. She was saying her rosary, a daily occurrence, and then Mary saw her find a chair and bring out a book. After her swim she went down to join her and together at 3 p.m. they watched the ship cast off and move away from its mooring.

On impulse, Mary asked, "Do you think I'm dreadful?"

"Mary! Goodness, why should I think you're dreadful?"

"Because I'm married, I suppose – though in an odd sort of way – and you must have known that my friendship with Gully was not platonic."

"Mary, all love has something of the divine in it. All love is God-given, God-driven even. Perhaps it's not always wise or even admirable or dignified but it's always an expression of our ultimate destiny. We are all called to love and to the love of God in the end. So don't reproach yourself for taking and giving it where you find it."

Interlude

I was deeply moved by the long story of my mother's shipboard love. I thought it a tender tale. I wondered if this kind and attractive man had been the benchmark and if Colin, my father, had never really come up to scratch, but when I asked her she denied it vehemently.

"It really was," she insisted, "the quintessential shipboard romance: short, intense but leading nowhere. I had two addresses for him that he'd given me – Naval Welfare, I think, and another one, but I can't remember. I tried to get in touch but I got no reply from Naval Welfare. He would have been in Singapore when it fell to the Japanese. So…" Her voice trailed off and I saw her pain, even then, fifty years later. So, shipboard romance or not, she had sought to contact him.

"So if it was all over, why try to get in touch? You must have thought there was a possibility of more?"

She didn't reply and I just smiled and let it go. She could say what she liked; I thought there was something special about her relationship with Gully. In fact, thinking about it, it occurred to me that although all the men in her life had been significant, among them Gully stood out.

Living in such close proximity, seeing her every day, I was always amused but sometimes a little embarrassed by her flirtatiousness. She became animated and teasingly chatty the moment a man appeared. The parish priest, her doctor, any workman – all became the object of an engaging coquetry.

"Mummy, Father Phillips has come to bring you Holy Communion! You don't need to flirt with him."

"Nonsense. I wasn't flirting, but even if I was, what harm?"

She deeply resented old age, which, she said crossly, had taken her by surprise.

I took her regularly to a local hairdresser, usually with my mother-in-law, and they sat side by side under beehive dryers. "How wrinkled I am," my mother would say sorrowfully, when eventually, coloured, washed, dried, and back-combed, she was shown the mirror. "Inside," she told me once, "I feel twenty-five." Actually, her face, wrinkled as it was, remained soft as velvet and as sweet. All her life she had perfect skin. Her hands, "little paws" she said, were, like her feet, tiny. Her fingers were short, so nobody noticed how slender they were. She laughed when she realized how her years had shrunk her. At ninety, she was barely four foot ten.

Our relationship had recovered from the bitter days before my marriage when, as she saw it, I had rejected her offer to make a home for me. Now the role was reversed: I was making a home for her. Although she clung to me emotionally, she remained as physically independent as possible, going along to the local shop and the post office, a tiny frail creature, stout-heartedly pushing her walker in front of her.

Her determination to stagger along rather than allow me to shop for her was strange, as long before she came to live with us she claimed to find walking any distance difficult. She had managed her local shops in Hove, so there was nothing wrong with her legs; she just didn't like walking. Clearly, once she was with me in Portsmouth she was not willing to give me total control of her life and I found that admirable. "Isn't she wonderful," people said. I looked at this diminutive creature after listening to the tapes, and thought of her courage in the lifeboat and could only agree.

As a back-up for when it might become necessary, I acquired a wheelchair for her, "just in case". She was both angry and dismissive. "This is the second time you've done this! I refuse to use it. You've wasted your time and your money." Her parting shot was, "Give it to Paul!"

This was a reference to an episode long before she moved in with us. One day she had phoned to say she would like to visit the Brighton dolphinarium. This was before the time when attractions of this sort had become unacceptable in Great Britain. I myself was dubious about the dolphinarium, but she had seen a TV programme about dolphins and was fired with enthusiasm. It was my son Paul's tenth birthday, so although I knew it was a fairly expensive attraction, I took him and another of his small schoolboy friends. My mother for once still seemed reasonably happy when what she thought was going to be a one to one with me was in fact a foursome. I knew we couldn't park nearby and would have to walk some distance. Her fury when I got the wheelchair out of the boot of the car was unbounded. "Mummy, we are parked over half a mile away. It's too much for you." She stalked ahead, rigid with outrage. Even then I was surprised how well she could walk if and when she had to.

"Can I sit in it, Mummy?" asked Paul eagerly, and laughing I agreed. This led to an unexpected situation developing. At the box office, the girl, looking with sympathy at my son sitting happily in the wheelchair, announced in the lowered hushed voice common with those who are uneasy with physical disability, "The little crippled boy is free." She then turned to me, her voice rising a tone or two. "You're free too, as you are his helper!"

"That's my mother," said Paul indignantly. "She's not a helper."

The girl was not fazed by this at all. "Well, she's pushing you, dear, and that qualifies her as your helper!" She turned to my mother. "And as it is Wednesday and Senior Citizens get full concession on Wednesday, you are free too." She beamed at her. My mother averted her face. She churned out the tickets, clearly delighted at the money she was saving us. "So it's only for the other little chap. That will be £5.00."

I looked at the tariff pinned up above the till. Children were £5.00, adults £10, and senior citizens £7.50. We should have paid £27.50 but only paid £5.00!

"Sit! Sit!" my mother hissed furiously at her giggling grandson, as we wound our way through dimly lit labyrinthine corridors lined with glowing aquaria in which strange multi-coloured exotic fish darted, and huge conger and moray eels and octopi writhed. Eventually we reached the dolphin pool. Assistants rushed forward and scooped us up. Then on the strength of the "little crippled boy" we got ringside seats and were drenched to the skin as a result by the leaping and splashing of those magnificent captive creatures.

After reproaching me for "cheating", my mother saw the funny side and laughed on and off all the way home. I always loved it when she changed from high indignation to appreciation of the ridiculous. It made me feel very close to her.

32

Temples and Snakes

"So are we going to look at snakes in Penang today?"

Mary put down the piece of toast she had been buttering and stared at Sister Maria Angelina in astonishment. "Good heavens! Why ever should we?"

"Ask Mr Hetherington. He says it's really wonderful: not to be missed."

Mary turned interrogative eyes towards the second purser.

"If you are going ashore here in Penang, you really ought to see it. It's a Buddhist temple, pretty enough, but it's the snakes thar are the real draw. They are pit vipers – very rare and worshipped as deities."

"But are they just crawling around and are they venomous?"

"I'm told they are quite sluggish and mainly nocturnal, so during the day they just coil around branches and don't bother anybody. But yes, they are venomous. Although I'm told they are de-venomed, they still have fangs. I've never heard of anyone being bitten."

Mary was not at all sure that a visit to a snake temple was an appealing outing but with no companion other than Sister Maria Angelina, who was clearly, as Mary told her teasingly, a "snakeophile", she had few, if any, alternatives. The nun didn't do shopping, or drinking in bars, or going to the beach, so sightseeing was what it was going to be. Mary hoped there might be other temples to enjoy, preferably ones free of snakes.

Mary had suffered some side-effects from her TAB inoculation – a sore arm and slight flu-like symptoms – and earlier had even considered staying aboard and resting. She thought of Gully and how much she was already missing him; he had been gone barely twenty-four hours. Going ashore without him seemed a dull prospect. But looking across the table at the nun's calm, smiling, sympathetic presence, it felt churlish to refuse to accompany her.

It had taken only twenty-four hours to sail up the Malacca Straits to Penang and the passage was lovely, the sea a deep emerald green. They were often in sight of land and small islands covered with lush vegetation. Fishing boats and yachts bobbed about, often perilously close to the ship, Mary thought.

They went ashore in a small cutter. At the last moment they were joined by the doctor, who smiled at Mary, she thought conspiratorially. She wanted to tell him that if he went on a bender, she would not be able to manhandle him singlehandedly back to his cabin.

"Do you mind if I come with you?" he asked. "I've seen the temple before but really want to see it again." He laughed: "I'm another snakeophile, I'm afraid."

He was the usual pleasant, calm medical officer and looking at him under the brim of her straw hat, she laughed silently to herself, seeing him as the rumpled drunken hobo swaying on the dockside only two days ago. She had an almost irresistible desire to ask him how often he stepped out of character.

The Hong Kong cable tram had been steep but the gradient was varied overall, whereas the little railway that took them up to the snake temple at the top of Penang Hill was precipitous, and halfway up the gradient increased to such an extent that passengers were obliged to change trains to cope with the difference. On either side of the narrow track, the foliage, sometimes heavy with luscious blossom, brushed the windows. It released a shower of pollen that made Sister Maria Angelina sneeze. At the top of the hill they had a wonderful view of the city below. It was a little cooler too. Mary had never been out with a nun before and glanced sideways at her, wondering how she coped with the heat, clothed as she was in a long-sleeved, ankle-length dress, headband, wimple, and veil. Mary, in comparison, in a cotton dress, sandals and sun hat, felt seriously underdressed.

"Sister," she asked impulsively, "are you sure you don't mind the walk? You've got an awful lot of clothes on. We can take a rickshaw." She was prepared to overcome her dislike of this form of transport to save the nun an unpleasant ten minutes. This was firmly and laughingly rejected.

"No, Mary, really I'm fine."

"But aren't you terribly hot?"

"No more than you and maybe even less. You get used to it, you know. Look at the Arabs in Africa, swathed in voluminous clothes and turbans. They do it to protect themselves from the sun and it seems to work very well."

They followed a meandering path, still climbing upwards. The ground was hot and dusty under their feet. Mary was glad of her sun hat. Tiny crickets leapt away in front of them and other unfamiliar insects buzzed and rustled in the undergrowth. Unexpectedly, a large, bright green lizard shot across their path. Mary gave a startled cry. The nun smiled unperturbed.

"The insects attract the lizards. It's OK, they don't want to nibble you!"

"Blimey!" Mary found her mouth dry with apprehension, although her brow was damp with perspiration. "Let's hope the snakes are sleepy." She wished she had refused this outing; reptiles were really not her thing.

The temple was larger than she expected but colourful, as all Buddhist temples are. A flight of stone steps went up to an open courtyard that led on under a glazed porch, beautifully tiled in red, blue and green, and then into the first part of the building. This was a sort of prayerful sanctum with an altar, followed by a succession of small rooms and other courtyards. The rooms were suffocatingly hot, with hundreds of candles and lamps. There were several devotees making offerings and praying, bowing before the altar.

"How lovely," said Sister Maria Angelina, delightedly. "It smells just like High Mass at home."

The light was dim, so at first Mary didn't see the snakes. Candles flickered and incense burners puffed out blue smoke that curled sinuously up to the rafters. In the interior rooms there were curious wooden structures like coat stands and coiled among them, sometimes two or three together, were the pit vipers – the object of veneration for the followers of this particular Buddhist sect. Mary peered upwards. The snakes, apparently indifferent to the presence of humans below, writhed occasionally and lifted their heads, as if looking for a more comfortable perch. Some were quite small, perhaps two or three feet in length; others were much larger. In the courtyard coiled in the branches of the small trees were many, many more.

"They are made sleepy by the incense." Mary was startled by the doctor's voice close to her ear.

"Are they indeed! I wouldn't like to put it to the test!"

"Don't you find them beautiful? Look at the colouration of their scales. Did you ever see such a vivid green?"

"Yes," replied Mary, repelled, "but look at that fierce, savage little head and the flickering tongue. Venom or no venom, I wouldn't like one near me."

He smiled. "Perhaps not," he said. Then he reached his hand into a tree and ran it gently along the length of a snake coiled around a lower branch. It moved sensuously beneath his caress.

"See that," he said. "It likes it!"

Mary couldn't tell if she was repulsed or fascinated. They wandered through the rooms and the courtyards. It was all much the same for Mary though: vipers and votives. She was relieved to be out in the fresh air.

Outside the temple a smiling pock-marked vendor was selling bottled juice and water, and the three of them bought some and sat on a stone wall to enjoy the view below. It was the first chance Mary had had to look around. From above she thought Georgetown, the capital of Penang, very beautiful with its tropical lushness. Distance, she told Sister Maria Angelina and the doctor, often lends charm. They agreed, although her comment made them laugh. On the ground immediately below their seat was a bushy shrub and Mary instinctively drew her legs up. She could imagine a pit viper crawling about below her.

"Where do the snakes come from? Are they caught? Who de-venoms them? Do they just arrive?" she asked.

Nobody answered and they sat in silence. Mary wondered fancifully if they were attracted to this sacred spot because they were sacred snakes. She had a mind picture of thousands of them crawling up the Malayan peninsular searching for the temple like reptilian pilgrims.

"Look!" said the doctor suddenly.

Jerked out of her reverie, she groaned, "Oh please don't tell me it's a snake." She felt she'd seen enough. He pointed to a branch on the shrub. There was a large pale green insect about three or four inches long. It had veined folded wings like a dragonfly. Its feelers were held out in front like a skinny boxer and its triangular head bore disproportionately large round eyes with tiny black pupils. As the doctor stirred the branch the creature swivelled its head to look at them, raising its feelers either in defence or aggression; Mary didn't know which.

"It's a praying mantis, Mrs Stewart. You will see plenty in India."

Mary looked at the insect. "It looks so alien," she said. Then, unexpectedly, she was overwhelmed by a piercing longing for home, for Dagenham, where the light was gentle and the climate cool. She thought of the canteen cat and the occasional nuisance of a fly or a wasp and where, if she wanted wild animals, she could go to Regent's Park Zoo. She thought – not for the first time – *I am so tired of all this brilliant colour, of this fierce tropical light. I want the pale, calm unremarkable landscape of Essex. I want to see my friends' faces again, drink beer in the Railway Hotel, go up to Petticoat Lane. I want to see Colin, hear him laugh and tease me and feel his arm around my shoulders. I want to feel married. I have been travelling so long. I am tired of the thought of India before I've even reached it.* It was a deeply depressing thought.

"You are very quiet, Mary. Are you alright? Have the snakes unsettled you?"

"Yes, yes, I'm fine." She gave herself a little shake mentally. "I was just thinking we don't see many praying mantis in Dagenham." She couldn't shake her mood off, remaining sombre and disinclined to talk. It was the same uneasy depression she had experienced when she had returned to the ship from the Peninsula Hotel in Kowloon. Perhaps it was something in the water, she thought, laughing a little to herself. In town they found somewhere for lunch and drank fresh coconut juice from shells, cool and delicious.

"Have you noticed," asked the doctor suddenly, "how varied colonial architecture is? It is as if each colonial architect wants to express himself in just a slightly individual way. It's almost the same and yet different. It's much more exuberant here than in Hong Kong. Although," he added, "I should think there's a blueprint for all Government Houses." He laughed deprecatingly. "But I'm just an American. What do I know?"

He was quite right, Mary thought. No one would ever mistake the buildings in Penang for those of Shanghai or Hong Kong.

"Not surprising," said Sister Maria Angelina. "Singapore and Penang are really Malaya. Shanghai and Hong Kong are China; completely different countries even if they are all governed by the British. I know you think we all look the same – Chinese,

Malayan, Japanese, Korean — we are all Asians, aren't we?" She spoke without rancour. "But of course we are all quite different so it's not surprising that even colonial architecture, wherever it is, has its own particular style, try as our masters would to make it all uniform."

Mary felt with some shame that she did think of all Asian races as looking the same. Also, because of her beautiful idiomatic English, she had begun to think of the nun as European. "You are quite right, Sister; we are dreadfully arrogant."

"No, no. Not that, but perhaps just a little thoughtless sometimes."

Sitting out on deck that evening, Mary asked her why she had become a nun. "Were you born into a Christian family?"

"Good heavens, no. I was born into a Taoist family who follow the directives of Confucius. My family were terribly distressed when I converted to Catholicism; it was even worse when I became a nun. Actually they haven't forgiven me yet although my mother was pleased to see me. We are not in touch at all at the moment."

Her face was tranquil but her lips quivered. "With God's grace, in time they will understand."

Her sadness was palpable and Mary was moved to see this gentle, sweet-natured woman distressed. She remembered Mrs Harrison in the lifeboat.

"'All shall be well'," she said, leaning forward and touching the nun's clasped hands, "'and all shall be well, and all manner of things shall be well!' A very dear and good person told me that when we were in terrible danger in the lifeboat. It is Julian of Norwich, I think. Mrs Harrison told me she was a medieval mystic."

Sister Maria Angelina smiled. "Your friend was right. She was a kind of nun too, but lived a solitary life. She had extraordinary visions and during one of them she heard Christ speak those wonderfully comforting words to her. Thank you for quoting her."

They went down to their cabins together and just before saying goodnight, Mary asked her tentatively if she would tell her a little more about Catholicism.

33

Colombo: The End in Sight

19 JUNE

*T*he despondency that had settled over Mary in Penang did not go away completely. As her long journey was drawing to a close she was dismayed that her feelings were not of excitement and anticipation, but rather of anti-climax. Had she gone through so much, she wondered, seen so many new things, visited so many places, only to have arrived at this flatness? She felt Penang had soured her, although deep down she knew that with Gully's departure, most of the enjoyment and pleasure of the trip had evaporated.

She decided not to go ashore at Colombo but to stay and keep Sister Maria Angelina company. But when the ship docked Mr Hetherington came to tell her that there was a message for her from the local May & Baker office. They were sending one of their staff to meet her, and she had a rendezvous for tea at the Galle Face Hotel. Apparently there were letters for her, Hetherington told her. The thought of the letters lifted her spirits so she set off for what she was told was the "oldest hotel east of Suez". The Galle Face was yet another impressive edifice. Mary was surprised how blasé she had become, thinking she had wined and dined, well "tea'd and caked" anyway, at almost every celebrity spot one might choose to mention.

Mr Da Silva was waiting for her in the lounge. He was a handsome Indian: slim, well-dressed with impeccable manners. Mary guessed him to be about forty. He didn't offer his hand but looked delighted when she offered hers and shook it warmly.

"Thank you, Mrs Stewart; thank you, so gracious." She was embarrassed to think that what seemed to her a normal greeting should be seen as an act of condescension, and wondered if she had given him "face". Did the Indians have the same concept of this as the Chinese? He asked her if she would like tea or a cold drink; she opted for tea. When it arrived, there was only one cup and saucer. She called the waiter back and ordered another, "and enough tea for two". Mr Da Silva smiled and lowered his eyes, whether from embarrassment or pleasure Mary wasn't sure. There was a short silence and then, as if recollecting himself, he took a packet from a leather attaché case and handed it to her. She opened it and took out four or five letters. Shuffling rapidly through them, she recognized her husband's elegant writing. Mr Da Silva smiled at her.

"Do please read them, Mrs Stewart. I'm sure you've been waiting a long time. I am so happy to drink my tea."

"I can wait a little longer," she said, tucking them into her handbag. She felt she owed him civilized conversation.

"You will love India," he told her. "The colour, the beauty, the spices. It is very magical. The people are so gentle, so polite, very civilized and of course so British in their hearts!" He said this with apparently no irony at all.

"The countryside is very wonderful," he continued, "and you must go to Simla or another hill station. You can escape the heat and really feel at home. Just like your Lake District, I'm told." She felt something close to dismay. She'd seen pseudo-Surrey in Shanghai and thought it very overrated. She hadn't wanted to come to India because it was so like the Lake District.

They talked for an hour or so. He asked eagerly about England, which, he said, he longed to visit. His ideas of the "old country", she learned, had been gleaned from the pages of Agatha Christie. He thought the fictional village of St Mary Mead, Miss Marple's home, "very perfect, so English. Of course I must learn to drink tea with milk!"

She answered his questions, she hoped with honesty, touched by his naïve enthusiasm. She was reluctant to disillusion him, so kept her replies very general. He expressed horror when she corrected his assertion that there were no snakes in England.

"But no dangerous snakes?"

"We do have adders; they are venomous, but small."

He looked shocked. "But Mrs Stewart, I assure you the smally, smally ones are the most dangerous. Our krait is one of the smallest but very, very naughty; very dangerous."

"Well, you won't find any krait in England, Mr Da Silva. Only one or two people are bitten by adders every year and all survive. Painful, but not deadly."

Really, she thought, she'd had quite enough of snakes. There had been a snake charmer outside the hotel when she arrived. The taxi driver pointed him out to her. The reptile appeared to be showing a clear reluctance to emerge from its basket, and in the end, irritated by its non-appearance, the charmer had upended the basket and tipped the snake out onto the road. It promptly coiled itself up and sank its head back into its coils. Its attitude was one of sullen resentment. No performance today, Mary thought. The charmer was eventually chased away by the hotel management.

Mary said goodbye to Mr Da Silva and on the spur of the moment wrote her Dagenham address down and gave it to him, "In case you are ever in England." He seemed quite overwhelmed but accepted it with dignified politeness. Again she had no expectation of him following it up. In this instance she was quite wrong and he did reappear with his beautiful wife, in Oxfordshire in 1963. He had a job at the Atomic Energy Research Establishment (AERE), Harwell, and rented a thatched cottage in Letcombe Basset. "Just like St Mary Mead," he told her gleefully.

She was back on board the ship in time for a bath before dinner. Her letters lay unopened on her bed. After her bath she dressed and it was only then that she turned to her correspondence. She opened the unknown ones. The first made her burst out laughing. It was a bill from the Ministry of Defence for her hotel in Montevideo. This charge, she had been assured by Lady Millington-Drake, would be assumed by the British government! She tore it up and tossed it away. The second was an itinerary for the final leg of her journey from Bombay to Calcutta. The third was another friendly reassuring missive from Dr Maxwell. Eventually she turned to Colin's. She was, in fact, apprehensive about reading her husband's letter. He had become a curiously amorphous figure in the ten long months since she had seen him. Occasionally she wondered why she had been so easily persuaded into marriage to a man she hardly knew. She thought of herself as sensible and level-headed. What crazy decisions people made when life was so disjointed, she thought. She sat on her bed and slit the letter open.

Very little had suffered from the censor's black crayon. It was a long, tender love letter full of yearning. He missed her and thought of her constantly, remembering their time together. He longed to see her. There was no explanation of his protracted silence. He expressed horror and wonder about the *Britannia*'s sad end and relief that she had escaped with her life. He was ashamed about his own easy existence, and had repeatedly requested a transfer to active service, only to be told his training work was essential. At the end he put something to make her smile. He and a fellow officer had bought a pair of fox terrier puppies – a dog and a bitch. He had chosen the bitch. The dog they named Rags and the bitch Bones. "She reminded me of you," he said. "Small, lively, affectionate, game for any new adventure. So I've attached your name to her. She's now 'Mary-Bones' and that's what everyone calls her; I hope you don't mind. She sleeps on my bed and wakes me in the morning by licking my nose. I shall expect no less when we next see each other."

She put the letter back in its envelope and then into her bag. She really didn't know what her feelings were. She could not fail to be moved by his words. His loving affection, so clearly expressed, touched her.

Over dinner she asked Sister Maria Angelina, "What happens if you fall out of love with someone? Or even if you've never really been in love? What then?"

"Well," said the nun slowly, "I can only speak for myself, but for me love is an act of will. It's nice of course if it's all hearts and flowers occasionally but really it's a conscious decision. You are attracted to someone, you decide to love them, and then you go with it. Parents love their children: babies are sweet, lovely, and cuddly and you don't give up on them, at least so I'm told, when they scream their heads off all night. Then they become quite repulsive young people, rude and difficult – well, my brothers did – and my parents still loved them.

"If you think about it, most of the great passions ended badly, didn't they? Look at Antony and Cleopatra and Romeo and Juliet. One can hardly bear to think of poor Anna Karenina, and as for Heloise and Abelard, it would not have ended so hideously if they had only kept their love platonic! Passionate love is all very well but so hard to sustain and to live with. So where do you go from there? You seem to have a good man, a loving man, perhaps not perfect, but who is? Carry on loving him in your heart, Mary, and maybe when you do at last see him, you will understand why."

Interlude

My mother's account of her long eventful voyage was nearly at an end. We had talked about it intermittently for months. She had been an animated and witty narrator. The tapes were chronological and, particularly the early ones, very revealing; the later ones were a little like a travelogue but always full of local colour and her own individual comments. That interminable journey became more immediate to her the older she grew.

Of her more recent life, she skated over the difficult middle years when I was in a convent, her marriage was crumbling, and her mental health was very fragile. That time she had put aside, buried really, and almost never referred to it. Yet I knew it had had a major impact on her fifties and sixties. In 1969 when I returned home, she had remade an acceptable life for herself but my arrival was as troubling for her as the adaptation to modern life was for me. I wanted to hear from her some account of what had gone on.

She was bitter about my father. She had supported him, she maintained, all her married life, both financially and socially. Initially I wasn't too sure about the latter knowing, according to her own account, she had not enjoyed service life. However, there were clearly moments when she had enjoyed it very much indeed.

I did remember her and my father giving parties, and there were photos showing her laughing and obviously having a good time.

"When I was sick he abandoned me. He found it difficult to cope with a wife suffering from mental health problems, as I was told they were."

"What do you mean? Do you mean you weren't ill? Tell me about this mental health problem. I knew when I was in Liverpool you'd been ill, hospitalized, treated."

She waited for a moment, then lit a cigarette, drawing on it fiercely. "My insomnia began in Germany after your brother was born. This was really the start of our married life together. Until then we hadn't really been a couple. I don't know why I began to sleep so badly. I think I was always worried." She laughed bitterly. "I worried mainly about money. I had a real horror of debt. Your father was quite irresponsible financially. Sometimes I'd sleep well but often my sleep was sketchy. Even when I'd had a reasonable night I never felt rested and I had a sort of stitch in my chest that frightened me. The doctors told me it wasn't my heart but a form of anxiety. Eventually, about the time you left home, when I was working at the AERE at Harwell, they gave me these wonderful tablets to perk me up."

She smiled grimly. "They reasoned that if I was sleeping badly, at least I would be on top of the world during the day. The result was amazing! I was full of life and energy, a new woman. I just felt wonderful."

I was saddened by her story. These pills, amphetamines, known as "Mother's little helpers", did exactly what they said, but they were highly addictive and over a period of five or six years, she became increasingly dependent on them. Bizarrely, her GP prescribed stronger and stronger dosages. I remembered her nervous agitation when she had come to visit me in France when I was a novice, and how thin she was. She never revealed to me the full extent of her illness; she may not have remembered; she may not have wished to remember.

Others gave me fuller accounts. Eventually, psychotic delusional episodes resulted in her being sectioned under the Mental Health Act and she had several treatments of ECT (electroconvulsive therapy). I never talked to her about this once she had told me about the disastrous consequences of the tablets. She preferred to talk about how she had rebuilt her life. One positive result of her hospital treatment was that she was weaned off amphetamines.

Her marriage collapsed, perhaps inevitably, after twenty or so years. Their Southsea house was sold, but with negative equity, so there was no money. She got a job working in the office of a repair garage, rented a comfortable bedsit in central Southsea, and found great comfort and pleasure in my brother and his girlfriend, later his wife, who lived nearby.

I still found it difficult to understand why she had become so friendless.

"Your father got there first," she said sadly. "I never felt I could put my own side of the story. And then you know a lot of my so-called friends dropped me. I saw people avoiding me. I was cut dead in the street on more than one occasion. I was Colin's mad wife."

Mental illness can have a stigma, even now, that is difficult to overcome for some people, and in the sixties it was certainly true.

My reappearance in her life, after my eight years in a convent, threw her again into turmoil. She had been made redundant which upset her but she had happily envisaged making a home for me, and thought that this was what I wanted too. Her bitter disappointment, when it was clear after a brief attempt to share accommodation with her that my aspirations were quite different, triggered another episode of depression and insomnia. This culminated in an accident, when she was injured in a house fire and was hospitalized with severe burns that needed skin grafts.

My own worry about her was compounded by guilt that I had not been able, nor indeed wished, to fit in with her plans for a mutual future.

She recovered from her accident and gallantly set about rebuilding her life yet again. John and I bought her a very pleasant studio flat in Hove and she tended the small patio garden with enthusiasm; it was a riot of colour. Her years there were years of contentment. She continued working into her seventies, running her employer's office with quiet efficiency. We never talked about her disappointment over my refusal to make a home with her. It was another example of her putting an unpleasant episode to the very back of her mind.

34

Bombay: Stopover

*I*t was with real sadness that at noon, standing on the quayside, Mary said goodbye to Sister Maria Angelina. She had become very fond of the quiet, sweet-natured nun and on this occasion promised vehemently to keep in touch. Addresses were exchanged, but as the small black and white robed figure disappeared into the crowds milling around, Mary felt as much a sense of loss as when she had said goodbye to Ted Boddle all those weeks ago. This was yet another new departure.

She stood for a moment surrounded by her luggage and looked around uncertainly. She had been instructed in Dr Maxwell's letter to wait for a Mr Marker, who she had been told, would collect her and take her to her hotel. Just as she had given up expecting him, she heard her name called and saw two people pushing their way toward her through the dense throng. Mr and Mrs Marker were a young couple about Mary's age, warm and reassuring, sensing perhaps that Mary felt alone and friendless.

Once in their car with the luggage following in a taxi, the Markers proposed settling her into her hotel and then driving her out to Juhu beach, a seaside resort about ten miles out from Bombay.

"We can have dinner there if you like. It's a beautiful spot. I have your train ticket for you: Mr Choppin sent it a day or so ago. I'm afraid you have a very long train journey ahead of you tomorrow. Over dinner I can give you some information about what Mr Choppin has organized for you in Calcutta."

Mr Marker seemed thoughtful and well organized. Mary was overcome with relief at not having to make any decisions about anything and fell in with their plans with pleasure.

The Rex Hotel was simple but clean – and she hoped comfortable; she felt the mattress and the pillows and was happy enough with them. The Markers said they would come back for her in an hour and she was left alone. Her room had a small balcony and she went out onto it to look at the throng below. She was enchanted. All the colour, noise, and smell of India greeted her. Across the road a group of women were gathered, laughing and talking, one with a small child on her hip. The vibrant colours of their clothes, the gold in their ears and on their arms, lent theatricality to their appearance. One could never have imagined that orange and purple or pink and yellow would go so well together, she thought. There were children everywhere. Leaning over the balcony, she looked further along the pavement, at the street vendors with their barrows. They wore baggy white trousers that she learned later were called "dhotis". From a distance they looked none too clean, and although most wore equally dusty white caps, one or two sported battered pith helmets. Their brown faces were wreathed in smiles. She wondered what they were selling and thought she would investigate later. The traffic seemed completely haphazard, and, as in other Asian cities, the modern jostled with the traditional. Once again the rickshaws were everywhere. The difficulty of traffic movement was compounded by the appearance of cows that shuffled into the road, ambling along at their own pace. Everybody and everything made way for them.

In the little reception area downstairs, waiting for the Markers to reappear, a waiter arrived and, unasked, silently presented her with a fruit drink. It was mango and she thought pineapple.

When she thanked him, he put his hands together as if in prayer, smiled at her, and bowed.

The Markers arrived as promised, and they went out together into the glare and heat of the afternoon sun. Mary was glad she had made an effort and washed her face and hands and changed her frock. Mrs Marker was elegant in a linen skirt and silk blouse. At Juhu beach they ate European food – some sort of grilled fish cooked over an open fire with fresh vegetables, served on large flat leaves. They risked one or two savoury pasties filled with spicy lentils that were pressed on them by the waiter. The heat of the day had abated and there was a comfortable little breeze. A crowd of small children gathered close by and stared at them with unblinking interest, giggling and hiding their mouths behind their hands. Mary smiled at them, thinking how beautiful they were with their huge brown eyes and black silky hair.

She felt relaxed and was enjoying the evening, when Mr Marker leaned forward and, looking earnestly at her, said, "Now, before I tell you about Calcutta, there are one or two things you might find useful about life here in general."

He looked so serious she wondered whatever was coming.

"Never, ever, under any circumstances, drink the water unless it has been boiled. Never have ice in your drink unless you are certain that that too has been made with boiled water. Never eat fruit unless it has been peeled or washed in boiled water. The Indians are used to it and have some resistance, but I am afraid we newcomers are still very susceptible to what we call the 'collywobbles' or 'Delhi belly'. Another thing: the natives are delightful, but bribes are the currency of the everyday. They don't ask for them; they just expect them. So apart from when you are bargaining for goods, always expect to pay over the odds."

"Even when you think you've got a bargain, in the market for example, you will almost certainly have paid too much," interjected Mrs Marker. She smiled deprecatingly. "It took me some time to realize that."

"So how do I know?" asked Mary. She felt despondency settle over her again. Petticoat Lane it certainly wasn't.

"That's where your bearer comes in. He's your servant, your factotum, if you like. He will protect you from others. He may steal a little from you and cheat you too, but he will prevent others from doing so."

"Do I really need a servant?" Mary asked, startled. There was a little uneasy silence. She turned her face and looked out beyond the beach. She thought of home and how she had bought orange boxes to make furniture for her flat. She thought of Colin running the vacuum cleaner over the carpet and of bringing home her own shopping in two string bags. "I've never ever had a charwoman or anything. This seems so unnecessary. I know how to clean, wash, and iron. Surely I don't need a servant," she repeated. Mrs Marker looked at her with sympathy.

"Certainly you do. You can't function as a European here without one. Believe me, it is so different from England. When I get home I don't expect to need a charlady or a gardener, but this is India. Anyway, all the middle-class Indians have them too. Your bearer is your houseboy. He will clean, cook, and iron for you; run errands, do your shopping and prevent you being cheated by the traders you deal with."

Well, Mary thought resignedly, *if it's normal I suppose I'll have to have one*.

"I do know how you feel," said Mrs Marker with some sympathy. "I was just the same when I came out, but actually they despise you if you don't have a bearer; they see it as a lack of personal dignity."

"How much do I pay him?" Mary made a last ditch stand against the idea of a servant. "Can I afford him?"

The Markers laughed. "Mrs Stewart, you could afford several servants if you wished. The usual rate is thirty rupees a month, which is about two pounds fifteen shillings."

Mary was shocked into an exclamation of outrage. "A month! Is that all? My God!"

"No, no!" The Markers spoke in unison. "India is cheap and that's a perfectly respectable wage for him."

"Anyway," Mr Marker interjected, "let me tell you about Calcutta and what Mr Choppin has organized for you. He has found a flat with a rather odd arrangement, but I think you will like it. It is in a very nice area."

"I know Choppin," said Mary with a sigh. "An odd arrangement means he has some plan to unsettle me. He is, I imagine, very put out that I have taken so long to get here."

The swift glance that the Markers exchanged confirmed her suspicion.

"The bedroom and bathroom are on one side of the street and the living room and the kitchen on the other." He cleared his throat. "But actually it's really very pleasant and with a bearer... ." His voice tailed off.

Mary thought it sounded very odd indeed but decided to say nothing. If it was completely unacceptable she could always find something better later, she reasoned.

After the meal there didn't seem to be any more to say. They strolled along the beach until the sun was well down and then the Markers took her back to the hotel, chatted for a while, then left her, wishing her well and saying they hoped to meet again. She thought them a very pleasant couple and their advice helpful. The first day in this new country had passed off well. She had had no time to miss her shipboard companions and once again, she reflected wryly, new events were slotting into the gaps left by the passage of the old. Back in her bedroom she repacked a small case for the three-day train journey, had a bath, closed the shutters, and went to bed. The mattress was lumpier than she had first thought but with the street sounds fading she slipped into sleep.

She woke suddenly in the early hours, disturbed by some unidentified noise and, reaching out, groped for her bedside lamp. She blinked in the light and peered about her. Sitting on the small chest of drawers under the window was a large rat.

It sat up on its back legs, looking at her, its whiskers twitching. She noted the pink ears and the front paws. The curled bare serpentine tail was repulsive but overall it was not unattractive. She stared at it blankly, wondering if she should scream. She looked around desperately for something that she could throw at it but there was nothing to hand. The rat, apparently quite unafraid, looked at her, Mary thought indignantly, as if completely at home. After a long pause the creature dropped down onto its front legs, then jumped onto the windowsill and vanished behind the shutters and through the slit of open window. She sprang up and slammed the window shut. Having peered gingerly under the bed to reassure herself that there were no others, she returned to bed and surprisingly fell asleep again immediately, waking next morning refreshed and ready for the last stage of her odyssey.

She wasn't quite sure how to handle the business of the rat but felt she ought to mention it, at least at the reception desk. Other guests might not be as sanguine about it. She was surprised with the equanimity with which they received this information, explaining that rats were a common feature but thankfully the snakes kept them down! She laughed aloud, wondering if this was meant to reassure her.

"It might have jumped onto my pillow," she pointed out.

"Oh no, Memsahib. It knew it was a bed."

The illogicality of this response silenced her, so she smiled and asked that her luggage be brought down and a taxi ordered for her.

35

Calcutta: Safely Arrived

$\mathcal{T}$he railway station was a seething, heaving mass of humanity. Mary thought she had never seen so many people crowded together in such a confined area. Men, women, children, porters, railway officials, beggars, and vendors all jostled for space, calling out to each other, shouting directives, searching for their luggage, fighting to get to the ticket office. The platform was filled with the acrid smell of the huge engine, still panting and hissing like some monstrous beast from its recent arrival. The driver with his blackened face was leaning from the cab to direct work being done to one of the wheels. Some carriages were being uncoupled in order for others to be attached, so there was a certain amount of shunting back and forward. The noise was unnerving.

Mary said firmly to the porter who had brought her luggage in, "Stay here, please, till I get back," and made her way determinedly through the crowd towards the ticket office. She was in a queue of about ten people, and there was a great deal of shoving, which she found unpleasant and even alarming. The train departure time was some twenty minutes away, but she needed to find her carriage and compartment. She had been told by Mr Marker to present herself to the ticket office where she would be given this information. Nobody seemed to be moving forward and she was just considering ignoring the queue and pushing in, when her elbow was pulled and a smartly dressed railway official said quietly, "Memsahib, Memsahib, please to come this way."

She followed him through the crowd to a door leading into a large air-conditioned waiting room with comfortable chairs. He held the door open for her and when she turned to ask about her luggage, he said quietly, "Your cases are here, Memsahib. They have been collected and before the train leaves, I will come to take you to your carriage."

"I haven't tipped the porter," Mary said helplessly. "I really ought to tip him. Can you do that for me?" She put some loose change into the man's hand, thinking foolishly that she'd no idea how much she had given him. He bowed and smiled and left.

"He'll pocket that himself," said a lean elderly European sitting in the corner of the room, who had been listening to the exchange with interest. He put down his newspaper and looked at her.

"It doesn't matter, I suppose. I meant to tip him too." She was irritated that she had been caught so unexpectedly in a situation where she hadn't known what to do. There had always been others with her before: Gully or Mr Hetherington, or even sweet Sister Maria Angelina, who understood local currency and advised her. She felt suddenly terribly alone. She sat down with relief and gratefully accepted the cup of tea that an attendant brought over to her. It was dark and strong and milk-less but she found it, despite its bitterness, refreshing.

"Is this your train?" her companion queried. He looked surprised.

"Yes, it is. Are you travelling on it?"

"No, mine is later."

After about a quarter of an hour, a loudspeaker announced the imminent departure of her train and the official returned and escorted her out onto the platform, which Mary discovered to her astonishment was virtually empty. A glance along the train showed it crammed full of travellers. She seemed to be the last passenger to board. As she followed the porter along the corridor to her compartment, she saw she was the object of what seemed to be surprise, even astonishment, which puzzled her.

Her compartment was spacious for one person, the bench seat comfortable, but having spent most of her travelling time in first-class accommodation, she saw immediately that this was not up to standard. The fittings were shabby and the washbasin in the corner was partially detached so that, as she discovered later, it rattled. The windows fitted badly and let in both dust and insects. The attendant was civil and as soon as the train left the station, he brought her more tea and very sweet biscuits made of rice and dates. Shortly after that he and another attendant arrived with a huge block of ice wrapped in canvas which they pushed out of her way under the bunk.

"For coolness," they told her.

The day passed quietly, although the heat, despite the ice block, became increasingly unpleasant. To occupy her mind, she wrote her diary and read again the A. J. Cronin book *The Citadel* that she had bought in Singapore. As it got dark, the attendant arrived to prepare her bunk and to bring her dinner. The food was so spicy she couldn't eat it and she looked dubiously at the carafe of water that accompanied it. Remembering the Markers' advice, she asked, "Has this water been boiled?" Disconcertingly he assured her it had, shaking his head at the same time. She later got used to the Indian custom of shaking the head to mean "Yes", but that day it confused her.

"Has it or hasn't it?" she asked crossly, only to get the same reply and the same head shake.

"I would like you to go and make me some tea please, and when the water has boiled, just bring me the water. Not tea, just the water that you have boiled. Do you understand what I want?"

"Yes, Memsahib, boiled water for tea." When he came back smiling, it was with a teapot filled with tea.

The bedroll, when she examined it, although covered with an immaculately ironed sheet, was stained and very thin. She put on her nightdress and dressing gown and set off up the passage for the lavatory. Passing other compartments where the blinds had not been pulled down she saw nothing but Indian passengers. Her belief that she was the only European on the train was confirmed the next morning when a smart and very pleasant inspector came to check her ticket. He said how honoured he was to have her on the train. The absence of other Europeans explained the surprise of the man in the waiting room at Bombay station.

"All your countrymen, people going from Bombay to Calcutta, travel in the 'Ice', Memsahib; it is an air-conditioned train, very comfortable, English food. But we are very honoured to have you with us. Please to ask for what you want."

"When we next stop," asked Mary, "could you get me some bottles of water, sealed bottles of water, and perhaps some oranges or fruit that I can peel?"

When they next stopped at noon, he arrived with mangoes and another fruit with an unfamiliar appearance, which he said were called custard apples; sadly, there was no bottled water. "This is a very small station," he explained apologetically. So there was yet more tea.

As the train travelled north the temperature rose and it became unbearably hot. The air circulated sluggishly and her body felt both clammy and feverish. She didn't bother to get dressed but lay on her bunk. The countryside they passed through was flat and featureless. If she lowered the blinds the compartment became stifling; if she opened the window, she was assailed by insects, smuts of soot and dust. The block of ice had melted; she assumed the melt must have found its own egress as the floor was dry. A small colony of ants had established itself in one corner but she felt too hot and too exhausted to do anything about it. She thought, *I'm letting the side down. This is not very British*. She did wonder what malignant imp had caused Choppin to book her onto this third-class form of rail travel when there was a much more comfortable option available. Then she remembered the Markers' mutual glance when she said her boss often did things to unsettle her. The tone in his one-off communication while she was on her Pacific crossing had led her to say to Gully and Sister Maria Angelina, "It's almost as if he thinks this long delay is deliberate on my part, just to annoy him."

Years later, she was to remember that train journey with bitterness and resentment. She felt it changed her relationship with her boss. He wasn't just a demanding eccentric; he was a man with a vindictive streak. Was he resentful of her adventures? Did he wish it had been him who had faced and overcome so much adversity and had such an exciting trip – so much more than he had ever seen? Did he wish that it had been him to be fêted and praised for courage and resourcefulness? They never discussed it afterwards, but recognizing that weakness, that flaw in him, gave her an ascendancy over him that she never lost.

On the morning of her arrival in Calcutta she had overcome her distress. She ordered hot water, washed and changed into a fresh frock, brushed and combed her hair into some order, put on her make-up, and was determined not to give Choppin any reason to believe she had found the journey anything other than pleasant. She tipped the attendant and the inspector, and thanked them sincerely for their care. She stepped down from the train and saw her luggage pulled along on a trolley. Then from out of the crowd on the platform, she saw her boss's saturnine face. He was smiling broadly and in that instant all her resentment melted away and she moved towards him, meeting smile with smile.

"Well, Frederick," she said, "here I am at long last." If he noted this first time use of his Christian name, he made no indication of it.

"Mary!" he answered, pulling her into a great hug and kissing her cheek. "Mary," he said – he who had always called her Mac

– "here you are indeed. At long last and only a few months late, welcome to Calcutta."

Then he took her arm and steered her out of the station and into the kaleidoscope of colour and the cacophony of noise that was the framework for her next adventure.

Epilogue

$\mathcal{T}$he tapes ended here. Mary's story ended. The Japanese attack on Pearl Harbor and the fall of Hong Kong and Singapore not six months after her arrival in India preoccupied her a great deal. She wondered and worried about Gully and his friends. What had happened to them? She never did find out.

Her husband Colin, my father, eventually got his transfer to active service and fought in the Burma campaign. He came to see her in India, when on leave. He had suffered from bouts of malaria and had been unwell. "He was thinner and tired and slept a lot," she said. She looked after him with tender concern.

She loved Calcutta but her own health in India was not good. Despite all her precautions, she was twice ill with dysentery and went to Mahabaleshwar, a hill station, after the second attack. There she recuperated in a nursing home run by nuns and during that time took instruction and became a Roman Catholic.

My father had a second short leave in April 1942 but in July of that year Mary was repatriated to England via South Africa. She was three months pregnant. Like a "homing pigeon" she said, she went north to Dunoon to have her baby, staying with her parents before returning to Dagenham with the child and moving back into her pleasant flat.

The tapes were an astounding revelation. They put my mother in a completely new light. I still thought her difficult and self-obsessed, but her undoubted courage and resourcefulness added another dimension. She had often lived her life with gusto, recognizing how fleeting, how transitory so many things were. She was not always wise and could be naïve.

She must have felt, in later life, that her world had become very unsafe. My father's shameful behaviour, abandoning her when she was most vulnerable, led to great bitterness. He was not a bad man, but weak, and a sick wife was not something he was prepared to cope with. Her psychotic episodes as a result of her amphetamine addiction, the consequence of medical mismanagement, were the precipitating factors in her general decline.

She remained true to her essential nature in remaking her life. I think unconsciously she felt she had a right to a certain egotism. Until we bought her a tiny flat in Hove, she had no champion to help her fight her battles.

She lived with us for eight years and died in 2003, aged ninety-three, in her own bed after a short illness, surrounded by her family. She lies in a quiet and peaceful grave. At her Requiem Mass my brother spoke movingly of "coming to say goodbye to this very old, very feisty Scottish lady".

Despite her peripatetic life, she never forgot her Scottish roots, nor lost her Scottish accent. Her coffin was piped into the church and the lament "The Flowers of the Forest" was played by the piper as we laid her to rest. She would have loved that.

I miss her.

Eleanor's own story can be found in...

Kicking the Habit

Kicking
the Habit

From Convent
to Casualty
in 1960s
Liverpool

ELEANOR STEWART

"Gripping, funny, poignant, and convincing."
Gervase Phinn

If you liked Call the Midwife, you'll love *Kicking the Habit!*

What makes a fun-loving teenager turn her back on a life of parties, boys and fun, to become a nun in a French convent? And what later leads her to abandon the religious life, to return to the big wide world and later marry?

At the age of 18, Eleanor Stewart goes to France to enter a convent. After four years of struggling with the religious life, she becomes a nun, and then trains as a midwife in a large inner-city hospital in Liverpool. While Beatlemania grips the nation, she attempts to coordinate the reclusive demands of the religious life with the drama, excitement and occasional tragedy of the hospital world. Written with honesty and affection, this is a wonderful and intimate portrait of convent and hospital life.

Published by Lion Books
ISBN 978-0-7459-5611-4

New Habits

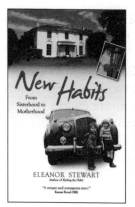

The sequel to *Kicking the Habit*...

When Eleanor Stewart abandoned her vows and her life as a nun, she found herself in the middle of the swinging Sixties – and soon joined in. Boyfriends, parties, and mini-skirts took the place of silence and restraint, as she pursued her career as a midwife and the men she met with equal commitment. Troubled by her relationship with her mother, and what she saw as a growing estrangement from her faith, she finally falls in love and settles down – only to discover her past catching up with her, as she faces infertility. But with her husband at her side, they battle to adopt two children. Will the dream of a happy family, that drove her out of the convent, finally come true?

Published by Lion Books
ISBN 978-0-7459-5668-8

Also from Lion Books...

Incontinent on the Continent

To honour a promise to her dying father, Jane takes her ageing incontinent mother to Italy. What could possibly go wrong?

Jane Christmas had always had a difficult relationship with her mother, but she thought that a mother and daughter trip to Italy could be the start of a whole new friendship. In this hilarious but poignant memoir, she discovers that it will not be that easy. Describing her mother as a cross between "Queen Victoria and Hyacinth Bucket", Jane struggles to build bridges with a woman she has always found a puzzle, while also trying to cope with her mother's failing health and increasing physical needs.

Published by Lion Books
ISBN 978-0-7459-6893-3